NESS
On Architecture, Life, and Urban Culture

D1520287

A platform developed
by Lots of Architecture
– publishers

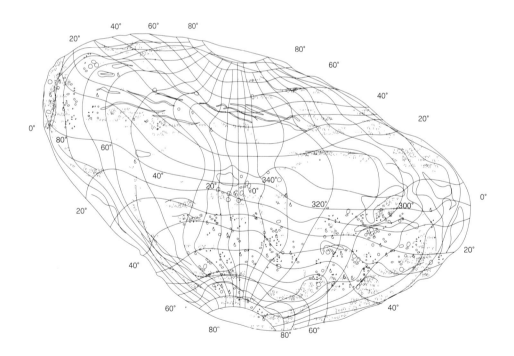

40° 60° 80°

20°

80°

60°

40°

20°

0°

80°

60°

40°

20° 0°

340°

320° 300°

0°

20°

20°

40°

40°

60°

80°

80° 60°

1

Our time
is about
radical
change

Cities are in constant growth and growth brings with it new needs. People are changing: the ways we live, experience, talk, think, and feel are in clear transformation.

Meaning, climate, economy, politics, space, relationships, education, languages, art, lifestyles, rules, genders, identity, fashion, contexts, revolutions, ecosystems, culture, communication, bodies, societies, and everything that once defined our modes of inhabiting this world have been in a process of dramatic and constant reformulation since the moment we first brought television into the domestic sphere.

Today, we understand that the complexity of our world, and the diversity of voices that compose it, have created a multiplicity of formal expressions, interpretations and desires that reflect the way we live, define, and inhabit our spaces.

Architecture has always had the power to become one of the utmost collective representations of an epoch: it materially manifests the ultimate milestones of the spirit of its time to confront the unbearable lightness of being.

2

That is why we created NESS: a media platform about architecture, life, and urban culture.

From philosophy to slang, words and the way we use them are being reinvented. That-ness, coolness, cuteness or otherness, are all signified to describe and innovate contemporary ways of thinking.

NESS is a suffix that gives an adjective or pronoun the possibility of becoming a noun. It invokes new ideas, senses, and meanings. It is playful, suggestive, and edgy.

Our company, Lots of Architecture publishers, finds value in imagination and invention as theoretical tools. They reinforce our active critical role in the formats we create for the dissemination of ideas, forms, images, debates, and dialogues as we search for cultural agitation, provocation, and the promotion of great and groundbreaking ideas.

We believe that proposals from all parts of the globe can contribute to the making of possible futures. We generate formats and contents that embrace the idea that architecture and the decisions we make about our built environments both condition and define who we are and how we want to live.

Lots of Architecture
–publishers
is a
megaphone,

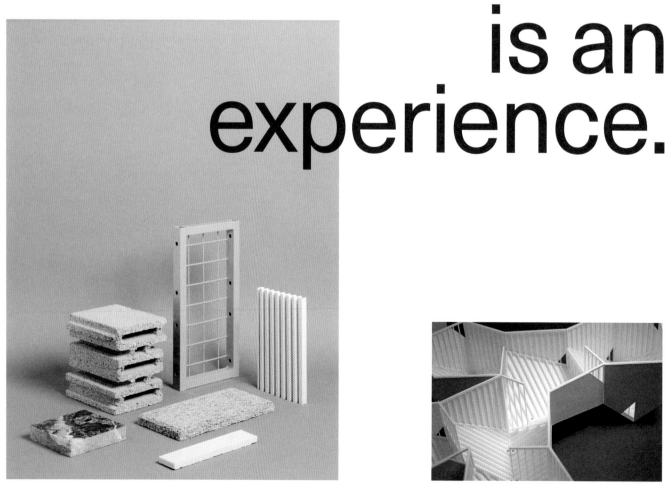

is an
experience.

1 – "Comet Halley 1P, *Cometa Halleyanus, Halleyscher*," analized and cartographed by Lena Wimmer for the book "Encounter." (see p. 50)   2 – Pablo Gerson shooting Lafayette Park during the Detroit research trip. Ph. Fernando Schapochnik (see p. 58)
3 – "'L'air pour l'air,'' performance at the Chicago Architecture Biennial 2017 by SO – IL and artist Ana Prvački. Ph. Iwan Baan (see p. 218)   4 – Texture samples for the Saint-Blaise Cultural and Sports Center by Bruther. Ph. Julien Hourcade (see p. 138)

It is an advocated way of thinking

6

about the capabilities of

design and architecture.

After a long creative and collective process, we are finally here, celebrating the value of talking, writing, editing, publishing, to subsequently start talking again.

NESS wants to be a worthy host: to entertain you and provide good company, but also to spark new ideas and present you with opportunities to reflect with no fear of being challenged. Certain crises offer chances to build.

That is how we experience our everyday work, as an ever-expanding learning process that is in constant motion, never fixed.

When we parse through this issue's first pages, we cannot help but feel proud. The amazing group of contributors that has written, photographed, participated in interviews, and generously shared their work with us, seem to echo our optimism.

NESS 1 is far more than we could have imagined when we started: it has already set the stage for an intellectually defying cultural project—one that we are honored to embrace. The artist Muntadas, our dear friend, often recalls the value of attention in perception. And that is what we hope to achieve: to gather, underline, point out, and interpret valuable work and worthy intellectual productions related to life, architecture, and urban culture.

So, welcome! Join our conversation and stay tuned,

Pablo Gerson &
Florencia Rodriguez

We would love to hear from you. Please send us your comments and opinions to hello@nessmagazine.com

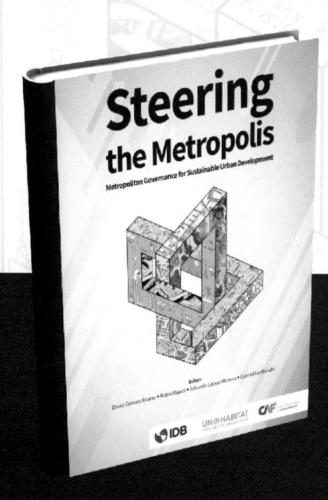

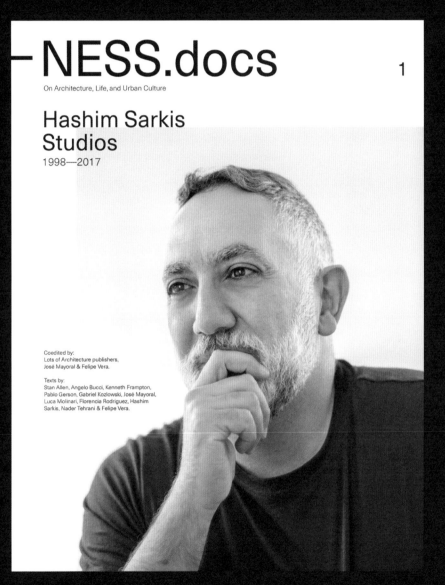

Credits

CHAIR & EDITOR IN CHIEF

Florencia Rodriguez
flor@nessmagazine.com

CHAIR & CHIEF EXECUTIVE OFFICER

Pablo Gerson
pablo@nessmagazine.com

EDITORS

Daniela Freiberg
dfreiberg@nessmagazine.com

Isabella Moretti
imoretti@nessmagazine.com

Lisa Naudin
lnaudin@nessmagazine.com

ART DIRECTOR

Diego Valiña
teoriaypractica.com

GRAPHIC DESIGNER & PHOTO EDITOR

Mariam Samur
msamur@nessmagazine.com

AUDIOVISUAL CREATOR

Natalia La Porta

PROOFREADER

Lisa Ubelaker Andrade

CONTRIBUTORS

Stan Allen, Emanuel Christ, Maurice Cox, Anna W. von Huber, Sharon Johnston, Steven Lewis, Enrique Ramirez, Camilo Restrepo, Javier Agustín Rojas, Fernando Schapochnik, Lisa Ubelaker Andrade, Jesus Vassallo, Lena Wimmer, Mimi Zeiger.

PHOTOGRAPHERS

Friederike Augustin, Iwan Baan, Pablo Blanco Barros, Federico Cairoli, Marco Carnevacci, Maxime Delvaux, James Ewing, Brian Ferry, Daniela Freiberg, José Gallego, Pablo Gerson, Laurian Ghinitoiu, Stefano Graziani, Miguel de Guzmán / ImagenSubliminal, Steve Hall, Brooke Holm, Julien Hourcade, Aslan Kudrnofsky, Natalia La Porta, Elizabeth Lippman, Kendall McCaugherty, Tamara Mehrer, Vincent Meyer Madaus, Magnus Pettersson, James Richards IV, Ola Rindal, Jessica Rocha, Florencia Rodriguez, Daniel Ruiz, Matthieu Salvaing, Mariam Samur, Philipp Schaerer, Fernando Schapochnik, Damir Zizic.

AKNOWLEDGEMENTS
We want to specially thank Diana Agrest, Joshua Akers, Joe Alcantara, Stan Allen, Juan Manuel Alonso, Wiel Arets, Iwan Baan, Christy Bieber, Louis Birdman, Brian Brash, Susan M. Burrows, Federico Colella, Florencia Colombo, Alecs Crespo, Dirk Denison, Ricardo Devesa, Marta García Collins, Mario Gandelsonas, Ana Gazze, Ignacio Gerson, Cynthia Leda, The Loeb Fellowship, Rodolfo Machado, V. Mitch McEwen, Florencia Medina, Carlos Mínguez Carrasco, Monte's crew, Dolores Oliver, Diana Ramirez-Jasso, Atila Rodriguez, Hashim Sarkis, Fernando Schapochnik, Jorge Silvetti, Christian Unverzagt, Sally Young, and all the contributors that with trust and enthusiasm accepted to participate in our first issue.

To Felix and Bruno, our little partners.

Published in 2018 by
Lots of Architecture publishers

1680 Michigan Ave. Floor 10
Suite 1000
Miami Beach, FL 33139
Tel: +1 (617) 674-2656
hello@lotsofarchitecture.com

ISSN 2574-8351
ISBN 978-1-7320106-0-4
Printed in the USA

ONLINE
nessmagazine.com
instagram.com/ness_magazine
facebook.com/nessmagazine
twitter.com/NESS_magazine

COVER PHOTOGRAPHY CREDITS

1   Texture samples for the Saint-Blaise Cultural and Sports Center by Bruther
    Ph. Julien Hourcade

2   Single-family house in Detroit
    Ph. Pablo Gerson

3   Enclosure models for the musicians for "L'air pour l'air" by SO – IL and artist Ana Prvački
    Ph. Courtesy of SO – IL

4   Relativity of Color and Side Table by LOT & objects of common interest
    Ph. Brooke Holm

–NESS

NESS is a product of Lots of Architecture publishers: an editorial platform dedicated to Architecture, Life, and Urban Culture founded by Pablo Gerson and Florencia Rodriguez in 2017.

FESTIVAL DE ARQUITECTURA Y CIUDAD

MEXTRÓPOLI 2018

RCR ARQUITECTES Premio Pritzker 2017 | Olot
VALERIO OLGIATI Premio Mejor Edificio en Suiza 2010 | Flims
STEFANO BOERI Director Future City Lab | Milán
PETRA BLAISE InsideOutside | Rotterdam
GO HASEGAWA AR Design Vanguard 2014 | Tokio - Los Ángeles
BAROZZI VEIGA Premio Mies van der Rohe 2015 | Barcelona

LLÀTZER MOIX Crítico de Arquitectura | Barcelona **JUAN HERREROS** Premio RIBA 2009 | Madrid
JOHNSTON MARKLEE Directores Artísticos de la Bienal de Chicago 2017 | Los Ángeles
MANUELLE GAUTRAND Premio Europeo de Arquitectura 2017 | París
FELIPE URIBE Arquitecto Director de +UdeB Arquitectos | Medellín
GUILLERMO HEVIA Premio Promoción Joven del Colegio de Arquitectos de Chile | Santiago de Chile
MAURICIO ROCHA + GABRIELA CARRILLO Emerging Voices 2004 | CDMX

JOSÉ CUBILLA Premio X Bienal Iberoamericana de Arquitectura y Urbanismo de São Paulo | Asunción
MICHELE LARÜE-CHARLUS Directora General de Ordenación y Planificación Territorial de Burdeos | Burdeos
KLAUS Arquitecto e ilustrador | Zaragoza **AARON BETSKY** Comisario de la 11º Bienal de Venecia 2008 | Taliesin
IÑAQUI CARNICERO León de Oro 15º Bienal de Venecia | Madrid **JUAN ROMÁN** Director de la Escuela de Arquitectura de Talca | Tal
HÉCTOR DE MAULEÓN Escritor y periodista | CDMX **ALEJANDRO HAIEK** Director LAB.PRO.FAB | Caracas
GERMAN VALENZUELA Co-fundador y ex-director de la Escuela de Arquitectura de Talca | Talca **Y MÁS...**

¡VIVE LA CIUDAD EXTRAORDINARIA!

17—20 MARZO | CDMX | @MEXTROPOLI
MEXTROPOLI.MX

Contents

Browser

The Dossier

Documents

Ph. Pablo Gerson

BETWEEN COZY HISTORY & HOMEY TECHNICS

Jeanne Gang and Nick Cave, "Here Hear", 2017.
Courtesy of Navy Pier. Ph. James Richards IV

Ph. Maxime Delvaux

Ph. Iwan Baan

BROOKE HOLM is an Australian/American photographer working across editorial, commercial, and fine art projects. Brooke's aesthetic and photographic sensibility has sparked interest from many corners of the world. This, combined with her instinctual love for nature, travel, and the desire to question the way things are, has largely contributed to her fine art practice and its constant evolution. While not shooting landscapes around the world, Brooke lives and works in New York City where she continues to collaborate with likeminded creatives on still life, architectural and design projects.

Brooke is the photographer for LOT and objects of common interest, in BROWSER.

MIGUEL DE GUZMAN is an architect and photographer. He founded ImagenSubliminal: Architectural Photography + Film based in New York and Madrid with Rocío Romero. ImagenSubliminal's photography has been published worldwide in print magazines as Architect, Dwell, El Croquis, Arquitectura Viva, A+U Japan, Domus, Casabella, Mark, C3, books, and newspapers. ImagenSubliminal: Architectural Photography + Film also collaborates with online media as Archdaily, Dezeen, Designboom, and Divisare. Their film work has been displayed at MAXXI Rome, Centre Pompidou Paris, and Architecture film festivals in New York, Los Angeles, Budapest, Santiago de Chile, and Seoul.

Miguel photographed SO – IL partners, in DOCUMENTS.

Contributors

DIEGO VALIÑA is an independent art director and graphic designer based in Buenos Aires, Argentina. In 2014, he established *Teoría & Práctica*, a platform that combines research, edition, and graphic design to explore the fields of architecture, arts, and culture. His practice produces printed publications, identities, websites, and exhibitions. He has lectured at the University of Buenos Aires between 2001 and 2008. He has taught the workshop *Leer para diseñar* since 2014. Currently, he is the art director of Lots of Architecture publishers.

Diego is the author of "The Making of a Typeface", in BROWSER.

LISA UBELAKER ANDRADE is Visiting Professor of U.S History and researcher at the Universidad de San Andrés in Buenos Aires, Argentina. She received her PhD in U.S. International and Latin American History from Yale University in 2013 and has published a number of articles on culture in U.S. international history, translated and edited several books, and is co-editor of the forthcoming Buenos Aires Reader (Duke University Press) with Diego Armus.

Lisa is Lots of Architecture Publishers' proofreader and the author of Detroit's historical chronicle, in REPORT–NESS.

In 2013, the College of Architecture at the Illinois Institute of Technology established the MCHAP to recognize the most distinguished architectural works built on the North and South American continents.

The Prize is awarded biennially at the masterpiece of S. R. Crown Hall, the organization's Chicago-based laboratory and mission control center. The recipients of the prize are named by a jury of professional architects, curators, writers, editors, and other individuals whose work has had a lasting influence on the theory and practice of design.

2016–2017

MCHAP

Mies
Crown Hall
Americas
Prize

Mies Crown Hall Americas Prize

Illinois Institute of Technology
College of Architecture
S. R. Crown Hall
3360 South State
Chicago, Illinois 60616, USA

+1 312 567 3610
mchap@iit.edu

www.mchap.org

 IIT College of Architecture
ILLINOIS INSTITUTE OF TECHNOLOGY

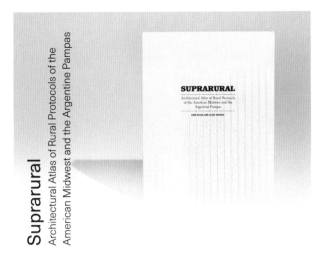

Suprarural
Architectural Atlas of Rural Protocols of the
American Midwest and the Argentine Pampas

AUTHORS: Ciro Najle and Lluís Ortega / PUBLISHER: Actar Publishers, 2017
EDITORS: Ciro Najle, Lluís Ortega, and Anna Font / PHOTOS: Pablo Gerson /
DESIGN: Ramon Prat / $34.95 — Available at actar.com

"The book provides an alternative approach to existing models
of relationship between the urban and the natural based
on palliative, decorative, or hygienist ethics. [...] The design
research was developed simultaneously in studios and seminars
taught at the School of Architecture and Urban Studies of
Universidad Torcuato Di Tella in Buenos Aires and at the School
of Architecture of the University of Illinois at Chicago by the
authors." (Extract back cover)

Landscape as Urbanism
A General Theory

AUTHOR: Charles Waldheim / PUBLISHER: Princeton University Press, 2016
DESIGN: Thumb – Luke Bulman with Camille Sacha Salvador / $45 —
Available at press.princeton.edu

"It has become conventional to think of urbanism and landscape
as opposing one another—or to think of landscape as merely
providing temporary relief from urban life as shaped by buildings
and infrastructure. But landscape has recently emerged as a
model and medium for the city. In 'Landscape as Urbanism: A
General Theory', one of the field's pioneers presents a powerful
case for rethinking the city through landscape." (Extract back
cover)

In our library

MCHAP
The Americas

AUTHORS: Pedro Ignacio Alonso, Wiel Arets, Luis Castañeda, Felipe Correa,
Kenneth Frampton, Fabrizio Gallanti, Jorge Francisco Liernur, Dominique
Perrault, Molly Wright Steenson, Pier Paolo Tamburelli, Horacio Torrent,
Sarah Whiting, and Mimi Zeiger / PUBLISHERS: IITAC Press and Actar
Publishers, 2016 / GUEST EDITOR: Fabrizio Gallanti / PHOTOS: Iwan
Baan, Ramak Fazel, Hans Gunther Flieg, Edi Hirose, Martha Rosler, Jeffrey
Schnapp, and Kazuo Shinohara / DESIGN: Mainstudio / $44.95 — Available
at actar.com

"This publication is an initiative of the Illinois Institute of
Technology's College of Architecture and its affiliated MCHAP
Mies Crown Hall Americas Prize, to recognize the most
distinguished architectural works built on the North and South
American continents." (Extract back matter)

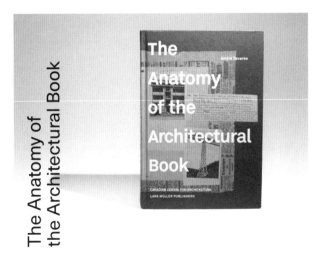

The Anatomy of
the Architectural Book

AUTHOR: André Tavares / PUBLISHERS: Canadian Centre for Architecture
and Lars Müller Publishers, 2016 / PHOTOS: Denis Farley, Michel Boulet,
Mathieu Gagnon (CCA) / DESIGN: Drop / João Faria / $49 — Available at
lars-mueller-publishers.com

"Architectural bookmaking has been exposed to disciplinary
debates, just as building construction has been exposed to the
charms of book culture. Examining the crossovers between book
culture and building culture makes visible the axes along which
architectural knowledge circulates through books into buildings
and back, from the celebration of specific architectural practices
to the production of unique books, using pages and print to
convey architectural ideas." (Extract back cover)

The Making of a Typeface

From Helvetica to Neue Haas Unica

DIEGO VALIÑA

Neue Haas Unica is the new version of a graceful and sober sans serif that we chose in the development of our editorial design and visual identity. This is the story behind the type.

ABCDEFGHIJKLMNOØP
QRSSȘTUVWXYZÆŒaáà
âäåãbcçdeéèëfgğhiíeìeî
eïejijklmnñoóòöõøpqrsş
tuúùûüvwxyzæœß&«»
1234567890$£†§.,:;!?'-()*

Helvetica was developed by Swiss designer Max Miedinger with the help of Eduard Hoffmann in 1957. Designed as an update of the so-called 'grotesque typefaces' developed in Germany in the late 19th century, Helvetica was increasingly popular. By the mid-seventies, it had transformed the written world giving a clear, modern look to magazine ads, subway signs, letterheads, and corporations such as Knoll, Panasonic, FedEx, Lufthansa, and American Airlines.

Helvetica's inventors, the Swiss Haas Type Foundry, originally commissioned Haas Unica in 1973. It was developed between 1974 and 1984 by André Gürtler, Christian Mengelt, and Erich Gschwind, who founded Team'77 Letterform Research & Design in 1977 as an independent partnership for typeface design projects.[1] They set out to mend common problems found in the 'grotesque typefaces' at the time. The work resulted in a comparative study and rigorous analysis of four major modern grotesque typefaces: Akzidenz Grotesk, Neue Haas Grotesk, Helvetica, and Univers. Haas Unica, which was predetermined for phototypesetting, was designed to be cool and neutral right from the beginning: sharper than Helvetica, warmer than Univers, and cleaner than Akzidenz. After dozens of adjustments, Team'77 documented that process

in "From Helvetica to Haas Unica," published simultaneously with Haas Unica's release. Where Helvetica's capital letters were blocky and tended towards a uniform width, Team'77 restored Haas Unica's capitals to more natural proportions. The designers balanced the thickness of strokes throughout the alphabet and tweaked spacing. The group concluded that Haas Unica had "tighter rhythm in upper case composition" and "improved readability especially for continuous text."

By the time Haas Unica was finished, the Haas Type Foundry went out of business. The typographic world was on the verge of an imminent shift: desktop publishing. The advent of personal computers made it possible to be more experimental with types; phototypesetting was quickly losing relevance. The Neue Haas Unica family is an extended, reimagined version of Haas Unica. It was conceived in 2015 by Toshi Omagari, a typeface designer at Monotype UK. He gave the classic Haas Unica a new look, adding weights, languages, and letters. Sophisticated letterforms, sober character, and economical proportions perfectly meet current digital and print needs. A 'cosmopolitan typeface' for today's discerning design needs. The Neue Haas Unica collection is our chosen classic.

1   Besides Haas Unica, Team'77 has produced the following printing fonts: Cyrillic Gothic (1974) and Alpin Gothic (1974) for Compugraphic Corporation (USA); Media (1976), Signa (1978) for Bobst Graphic (Lausanne) and Autologic (USA); and Avant Garde Gothic Oblique (1977) for ITC (USA).

"New Spring, Miami" by COS & Studio Swine was an interactive installation at Design Miami/ 2017. The work comprised of a central, tree-like sculpture that emitted mist-filled blossoms. It was presented at the Temple House, an Art Deco building in South Beach.

Installation view at the Temple House. Ph. Courtesy of COS.

COS X Studio Swine

"New Spring, Miami" is a collaboration between COS and Studio Swine.
6 –10 December 2017, Design Miami/, Florida.

Teaser. Ph. Courtesy of COS.

COS is a brand for women and men who like modern, functional, and considered design. Committed to timeless design and innovation, COS supports the arts through collaborations with artists, galleries, and creative studios. On this occasion, the brand chose to partner with Studio Swine (Super Wide Interdisciplinary New Explorers), co-founded by Japanese Architect Azusa Murakami and British Artist Alexander Groves.

Design Miami/, a global forum for design, housed the second edition of the "New Spring" series. The first installation was shown in April 2017 during *Salone del Mobile* in Milan, where it was awarded with the "Most Engaging Exhibition" prize. Each work in this series is site-specific, responsive to its environment, and ephemeral.

"New Spring, Miami" responded to both the environment of Miami and the curvilinear, Art Deco location. Each blossom was filled with one of five scents inspired by Florida and its flora. Studio Swine said of the installation, "We wanted to encapsulate a lifespan of emotions in an instant, to create a multisensory experience that was fleeting, but in its time evokes joy and vitality, if only to remain as a memory. New Spring, Miami couples this ideal with the environment it inhabits; energized by the inspiration the city and the remarkable style it has given us."

Studio Swine also designed a concept shop, which drew inspiration from the installation and that housed a tonal selection of COS pieces specially chosen by Creative Director, Karin Gustafsson. The edit was inspired by the translucent, almost-there nature of the blossoms, while reflecting the tactility of different materials used in COS collections.

We edit magazines
We edit books
We edit films
We edit websites
We edit brochures
We edit posters
We edit fanzines
We edit boogazines

CONTACT US TO TALK ABOUT YOUR PROJECT
HELLO@LOTSOFARCHITECTURE.COM

The   Art

Nine installations that rocked 2017 by questioning, claiming, resisting, or presenting social conflictive issues that reflect contemporary world concerns.

DANIELA FREIBERG

Part of today's art scene is echoing and critically amplifying the phenomena of our time. Some of the most significant international venues and events held last year hosted works by artists and architects who addressed topics that, together, form a collective agenda of debate on social emergencies and global transformations.

This dispersed and eclectic group is using artwork to make visible fundamental questions of our time, such as mass displacement and migration. One key issue is what has been termed the 'refugee crisis.' These works contend with actions that encourage civic engagement, or discuss refugees' temporary dwellings, as is the case in Hiwa K and Olafur Eliasson's proposals. María Verónica Machado's installation brings up another pertinent issue: the idea of borders, and specifically that of Mexico and United States. The issue has drawn special attention, and particularly so in the aftermath of Donald Trump's election.

In another discussion regarding the dwelling, is an intimate exploration of the shared home that aims to conjure an understanding of Fien Muller and Hannes Van Severen's family stories, daily routines, personal style, and network of friends; the work creates the essence of home and homecoming in an Airbnb commission.

Aamu Song & Johan Olin, founders of COMPANY, highlight the hidden processes of design research as related to manual versus mechanized production with their atypical exhibition at Storefront for Art and Architecture.

Plastique Fantastique's temporary, monumental, soft, and transparent new scenario challenges our perception. Represented on a site-specific project integrated into its environment, this installation considers the peculiar position of every single tree in a Dutch forest.

Pierre Huyghe's public sculpture project draws attention to different interdependent processes taking place within a very large hall. Situations and environments are produced to allow transformations where biological life, real and symbolic architecture, are fused into a precarious symbiosis.

In two other works, technology is applied to matters of everyday life: environmental issues and open source frameworks are related in C+ arquitectos's project, which utilizes monitoring devices that aim to make air pollution visible, something that is usually reduced to figures and percentages. Digital and data are also present in an installation that questions public space in the era of surveillance by brilliantly placing guests in the position of both the observed and the observer. In what may seem like a 21st century interpretation of Orwell's "1984," Herzog & de Meuron and Ai Weiwei's work makes it impossible for visitors to hide their locations.

of   Denunciation

Ph. Damir Zizic

Green light – An artistic workshop

MAY – NOVEMBER
2017

OLAFUR ELIASSON, in collaboration with Thyssen-Bornemisza Art Contemporary (TBA21). 57th International Art Exhibition *La Biennale di Venezia* Viva Arte Viva 2017, Italy.

Growing out of the communal ideals of the artist's studio, Green light is thought of as a welcoming act. It was conceived in response to the present challenges arising from mass displacement and migration and it encourages civic engagement. In the ongoing series of Green light workshops, hosted by various institutions around the world, asylum seekers, refugees, and members of the public construct green light lamps and take part in an accompanying educational program conceived by TBA21, in dialogue with Eliasson. Titled "Shared Learning," offers practical training and education—daily language courses, job training, psychological counseling and legal advice, music and video workshops, artists' interventions, seminars, and lectures. The events explore perspectives on migration, citizenship, statelessness, arrival, memory, and belonging, eliciting exchanges of knowledge, experiences, and values.

On this occasion, forty individuals from countries including, Nigeria, Gambia, Syria, Iraq, Somalia, Afghanistan, and China, have signed up as participants through nine local partnering NGOs, all based in Venice. They take part in the workshop as well as the extensive Shared Learning program, which offers free access to all its activities, for a maximum of two months. The participants lead the daily lamp-building workshops, acting as hosts in the Green light space and engaging with the biennale visitors. Located in the Central Pavilion, is a space of individual and collective 'world-making.' By presenting a multilayered concept of hospitality that encompasses a wide variety of people—an artist, his studio, the participants, partnering NGOs, the visitors, etc.—Green light tests alternative models of community.

OLAFUR ELIASSON (Denmark-Iceland), works in a wide range of media, including installation, painting, sculpture, photography, and film. Since 1997, his solo shows have appeared in major museums around the world. Established in 1995, his studio today includes craftsmen, architects, archivists, administrators, and cooks. In 2014, Eliasson and S. Behmann founded Studio Other Spaces, an office focusing on interdisciplinary and experimental building projects in public space. Together with engineer F. Ottesen, Eliasson founded the social business Little Sun in 2012, a global project that produces and distributes solar-powered products for use in off-grid communities and spreads awareness about the need to bring sustainable energy access to all.

Ph. Daniela Freiberg

When We Were Exhaling Images

JUNE – SEPTEMBER
2017

HIWA K, in collaboration with the Diplom Degree Programme in Product Design, Prof. Jakob Gebert, Kunsthochschule Kassel: Thomas Buda, Arne Dohrmann, Olga Turiel Dorofeeva, Ferdinand Fach, Theresa Herrmann, Verena Hutter, Hedda Korthals, Jasper Ohainski, Carlos Platz, José Manuel Schloss, Mona Schmidt, Philipp Thomas, and Jennifer Witulla. Documenta14. Friedrichsplatz, Kassel, Germany.

The Berlin-based Kurdish-Iraqi artist created, together with students, an installation that uses vitrified clay pipes (used for canalization), laminated beams, furniture, and various objects to recall the temporary dwelling of refugees. As the artist commented in an interview, people fleeing the port of Patras in Greece had to spend long periods of time in similar 'houses.' He considers the exhibit a broader reflection on poverty, capitalism, and what happens when a person no longer has room for their belongings; a symptom of our society.

Hiwa K does not consider the work to be art, but a reality; he believes that he, himself, as an artist, can only express the problem. But he suggests that showing in Kassel is poignant: Documenta may constitute a peaceful and open gesture, but there is also a large industry for weapons in the city, which produces and exports to other countries.

Ph. Friederike Augustin

HIWA K (Kurdistan-Iraq) graduated from high school in Iraq and continued his self-education meeting different intellectuals, visual artists, musicians, and theater artists; he moved to Germany at the age of 25. Hiwa K's work escapes normative aesthetics but gives a possibility of another vibration to vernacular forms, oral histories, modes of encounter, and political situations. Many of his works are characterized by a strong collective and participatory dimension, and have to do with the process of the teaching and learning systems and an insistence on the concept of obtaining knowledge from everyday experience.

After ALife Ahead

PIERRE HUYGHE. Münster's Skulptur Projekte 2017, Münster, Germany.

Ice rink concrete floor; Sand, clay, phreatic water; Bacteria, algae, bee, chimera peacock; Aquarium, black switchable glass, conus textile; Incubator, human cancer cells; Genetic algorithm; Augmented reality; Automated ceiling structure; Rain; Ammoniac; Logic game.

The French artist has developed a time-based bio-technical system in a former ice rink that closed in 2016. This involved bio–and media–technological intervention and required extensive architectural deconstruction and reconstruction. All the processes taking place within the very large hall are mutually interdependent: some are determined by the HeLa[1] cell line, in a constant process of division in an incubator. Among its various effects, the cells' growth triggers the emergence of augmented reality shapes. Variations in a *Conus* textile[2] pattern change the spatial configuration: for example, the opening and shutting of a pyramid-shaped window in the ceiling of the hall.

Digging into the earth transforms the ground into a low-level hilly landscape. In some spots, concrete and earth, layers of clay, styrofoam, gravel debris, and ice-age sand are found as far as a few meters underground, interspersed with leftover surfaces. This space is inhabited, for instance, by algae, bacteria, beehives, and chimera peacocks. Biological life, real and symbolic architecture and landscapes, visible and invisible processes, and static and dynamic states are all fused into a precarious symbiosis.

1   HeLa is a cell type in an inmortal cell line used in scientific research. it is the oldest and most commonly used human cell line. The line was derived from cervical cancer cells taken on 8 February 1951 from Henrietta Lacks, (initials for the acronym) a patient who died of her cancer on 4 October 1951. They can be cultivated in the laboratory constantly.

2   Conus textile is a venomous species of sea snail, a marine gastropod mollusk in the family *Conidae*.

PIERRE HUYGHE (Paris; lives in New York) works, often present themselves as complex systems characterized by a wide range of life forms, inanimate things, and technologies. His arranged organisms combine not only biological, technological, and fictional elements, but also produce an environment for interaction between humans, animals, and non-beings as well as unicellular organisms or viruses. Huyghe's constructed situations are reminiscent of biospheres, where laws apply that are different than those found in nature: structural parameters for changes as well as phenomena like swarm behavior and cluster development are used, but, in the end—as with any other artistic material—these prove to be the final limits of the will to make new possibilities happen.

Ph. Ola Rindal

Ph. Jessica Rocha - Courtesy of the Fundación del Centro Histórico.

La 'política' del límite – 'Politics' of the limit

JUNE – OCTOBER
2017

MARÍA VERÓNICA MACHADO. Fundación del Centro Histórico through Casa Vecina and San Francisco atrium. CDM, Mexico.

This installation seeks to blur the idea of the frontier and the border as a site of separation, and turn it into a meeting place. It was built upon a drawing of the border line between Mexico and United States, laid in the San Francisco atrium, using more than a thousand three-meter tall PVC pipes that transform the trace of a territorial limit into an interactive and permeable space. Phrases written on vinyl, manuscripts, or printed in braille, intervene the pipes and approach, from different perspectives and experiences, the concepts of 'border' and 'limit.'

To generate and compile the phrases written on the pipes that make up the installation, the artist immersed herself in bibliographical research and became familiar with institutions and projects in Mexico and the United States that deal with problems that arise from the border in different ways—in conceptual terms, as well as its geographical-territorial elements and perception.

Ph. Courtesy of the Fundación del Centro Histórico.

MARÍA VERÓNICA MACHADO PENSO (Maracaibo, Venezuela) is a transdisciplinary artist, architect, and teacher-researcher in contemporary art, architecture, and design. She investigates and develops her work on subjects that transgress the traditional logics of these three disciplines; she works out of a laboratory of research that combines art and science.

Ph. Marco Carnevacci – Plastique Fantastique

Loud Shadows | Liquid Events

9 – 18 JUNE
2017

KATE MOORE, THE STOLZ, LEINEROEBANA AND PLASTIQUE FANTASTIQUE. Oerol Festival, Terschelling, The Netherlands.

The proposal is a collage made by artists that come from different backgrounds: dance, music, and architecture. The team has been assembled as an experiment by Kees Lesuis—artistic director of the OEROL Festival—to conceive a unique performance on the occasion of the 2017 festival's 2017 edition.

The temporary space of Plastique Fantastique is monumental, yet mobile, soft, and transparent. Its ephemeral skin influences the surroundings as much as its inner space offers a lucid view outward. It is a magical place to merge dance, music, and nature—challenging our perception.

The architecture of Loud Shadows | Liquid Events is presented in four different stages and designed by taking into consideration the peculiar position of every single tree of an area within the Formerum forest, on the island of Terschelling. Each element of this site-specific project is integrated into its environment: the first transparent spherical stage is pierced by a tree, while the second stage is squeezed between tree branches and comes under the projection of their shadows. The ring connecting the two stages loops around pine and oak trees creating the third stage in its void. The fourth stage is the forest around the installation.

Inside this constellation, the audience is free to circulate and choose its place. These movements are encouraged by the musicians and dancers, who are playing and performing simultaneously through the different stages. The composition is affected by unpredictable natural elements like birds singing, leaves rustling, wind gusts or rain drops, thus making each performance unique.

PLASTIQUE FANTASTIQUE is a platform for temporary architecture which samples the performative possibilities of urban environments. Established in Berlin in 1999, it specializes in creating pneumatic installations as alternative, adaptable, low energy spaces for temporary and ephemeral activities.
PLASTIQUE FANTASTIQUE: Marco Canevacci, Yena Young (Architecture / Scenography), Antonia Joseph, Stephanie Grönnert, Julia Lipinsky (Production, Lorenzo Soldi , Maria Turik, Carsten Reith (Terschelling team). LEINE ROEBANA: Andrea Leine, Harijono Roebana, Tim Persent, Uri Eugenio, Luana van Eekeren, Mark Christoph Klee, Stéphanie den Blanken. THE STOLZ QUARTET: Marieke Schut, Jellantsje de Vries, Lidy Blijdorp, Sabine Oldenburg. KATE MOORE (Composer). OEROL FESTIVAL: Kees Lesuis, Aline de Jonge, Alma Lindenhovius, Ada Plinck, Marelie van Rongen, Antoine Bronkhorst.

Temple of Manufacturing

JUNE – AUGUST
2017

COMPANY / AAMU SONG & JOHAN OLIN. Curators: Eva Franch i Gilabert & Carlos Mínguez Carrasco. Soundtrack: Tuomas Toivonen Storefront for Art and Architecture, New York, United States.

Ph. Miguel de Guzmán / ImagenSubliminal

This installation worships the making of things. The temple brings together ten years of Secrets, an art project in which Aamu Song and Johan Olin look into traditional manufacturing, collaborate with the makers, and, together, create new items. Temple of Manufacturing premieres the latest of their Secrets series: Secrets of USA. It is a collection of items created with Amish makers in Pennsylvania's Amish country.

After ten years of meeting with great makers, the authors still wonder what this making is all about: it is not about money nor keeping traditions—maybe it is a belief.

At Storefront, COMPANY presents its own Temple of Manufacturing, an installation that reflects the feeling of sacredness that the duo encountered while visiting spaces of production all over the world. Raw materials, drawings, objects, designs, and process documents are presented alongside a series of frescoes painted *in situ* that narrate some of the journeys, topics, and works that structure their research.

Exhibit objects are conceived and produced as composite figures from the office's own design methods and their trips to Japan, Russia, Finland, Estonia, as well as to the Amish communities of Pennsylvania. Part artist's travel log, part sanctuary for the maker's masters, and somewhere between an archive, an exhibition, and a store (the ultimate temple of contemporary capitalism) the installation reflects upon "the aura of the work of art" (in this case, the design object), and the hidden processes of design research as related to manual versus mechanized production.

COMPANY, formed by Aamu Song and Johan Olin, is an art and detective agency from Helsinki, Finland, that has been discovering manufacturing secrets worldwide for over a decade, working as artists, designers, and producers, and running their own shop (Salakauppa) in Helsinki.

Yellow Dust

SEPTEMBER – NOVEMBER
2017

C+ ARQUITECTOS / IN THE AIR (NEREA CALVILLO WITH RAÚL NIEVES, PEP TORNABELL AND YEE THONG CHAI, EMMA GARNETT, MARINA FERNANDEZ). Seoul Biennale of Architecture and Urbanism, South Korea.

A three-dimensional water vapor canopy, Yellow Dust is a sensing and sensuous infrastructure that monitors, makes visible, and partially remediates particular matter in the air through variable clouds of yellow mist. Composed by 'Do It Yourself' sensors installed specifically for this occasion and using off-the-shelf construction systems, it aims to contribute to collective forms of making air pollution visible. In contrast to scientific and policy-making versions of air monitoring devices, which are invisible and for which sensing is only about the data, Yellow Dust engages with the toxicity of the city by opening up the monitoring process in various ways: revealing the monitoring technology and its measurements, communicating the quality of air pollution not through screens or numbers, but through a sensuous experience with the data, and conditioning the environment by humidifying and cooling. It also provides the information to replicate the project in other contexts, as an open source urban infrastructure.

Ph. Daniel Ruiz

Specialized in new technologies as design tools, C+ has designed architecture projects and contemporary art exhibitions in Spain, Chile, and Serbia. Research projects oriented towards data visualization and cartographies have been developed in workshops at international universities and medialabs including Invisible Cartographies, In The Air, Kitchen Budapest, Museum of Contemporary Art Chile and exhibited at international venues, such as the Canadian Centre of Architecture.

Ph. Elizabeth Lippman

A Wild Thing

FIEN MULLER AND HANNES VAN SEVEREN. Commissioned by Airbnb. Design Miami/ 2017

This installation is an intimate exploration of the shared home. The space is a precise replica of the designers' living room in Ghent. Their furniture, artworks, books and other objects will be on location in their 'home away from home', a special opportunity for visitors to experience how they live. Interactive lightboxes with recorded scenes from their living room windows will transport visitors to their home in Belgium, immersing visitors in their local surroundings as well as their home. Simultaneously, the design duo has shared their home in Ghent on Airbnb.

Known for their creation of beautiful pieces of furniture and art, with this collaboration the office intends to share the deeper meanings that exist for treasured objects at home—which they label Wild Things. Using directional sound, narratives from their lives have been paired with selected items within the living room, creating a highly immersive installation and illustrating the invisible connection between hosts and guests—a truly Airbnb experience. Each narrative is a personal anecdote, reflecting the meaningful connections they each have with the objects on display. A painting by Hannes' grandfather, noted artist Dan Van Severen, is juxtaposed with a chair made by the couple's young daughter. Ambient sounds of the fireplace and the family dinner table are interspersed with sculpture, important books and other artworks— playing on the contrast between high design and the sentimental keepsakes that make up their home.

The installation aims to conjure an understanding of Muller Van Severen's family stories, daily routines, personal style, and network of friends, creating the essence of home and homecoming in a public space.

MULLER AND VAN SEVEREN founded their studio in 2011. They have won prestigious awards and their work has been exhibited in renowned galleries and museums in Belgium, London, Berlin, Milan, Copenhagen, Paris and New York. The duo explores the boundaries between art and design in a contemporary and innovative way and adopts an inventive and imaginative approach. They are constantly looking for new ways to make furniture more interesting from a sculptural point of view, without losing track of its functionality. They succeed in adding a personal, fresh new touch to major historical art and design movements. Their design method has an intuitive, spontaneous, authentic, and sincere feel about it.

Hansel & Gretel

JACQUES HERZOG, PIERRE DE MEURON, AND AI WEIWEI. Co-curated by Tom Eccles and Hans-Ulrich Obrist.
Commissioned by Park Avenue Armory, New York, United States.

This site-specific commission examines the changing nature of public space in the era of surveillance. The immersive, interactive installation, fills the Armory's Wade Thompson Drill Hall and extends into the first floor of the Head House, creating an eerie landscape permeated by modern-day surveillance. Placing visitors in the position of the observed and the observer, the multilayered work submerges audiences in an environment where their every movement is tracked and monitored. Visitors make their way through the Armory's bunkers and are plunged into darkness. As they navigate a disorienting terrain, their movement is recorded by infrared cameras, broadcast to a global online audience, and fed back into the installation. A white light follows the path of each individual across the Drill Hall, creating a visual record of visitors' movements before vanishing into the darkness behind them. With each step, the visitors' image is projected back onto the floor, becoming interrupted by shadows formed by surveillance drones that periodically survey the Drill Hall. The experience inverts the fairytale of Hansel & Gretel—instead of purposively leaving a trail to avoid getting lost, the surreptitious tracking of visitors makes it impossible to hide their location.

Visitors transition into the role of the observer when entering the Head House. This 'surveillance laboratory' simultaneously serves as a covert monitoring hub that makes participants cognizant of the extent to which they were being watched as well as a forum for visitors to discuss the ethics and societal impact of the growing culture of surveillance.

JACQUES HERZOG AND PIERRE DE MEURON (Basel). Pritzker Prize-winning architects established Herzog & de Meuron in Basel in 1978, having completed over 400 projects, including the copper-wrapped Signal Box in Basel, the Dominus Winery in Napa Valley, the Walker Museum in Minneapolis, the Allianz Arena in Munich, the Caixa Forum in Madrid, the Tate Modern, the Chinese Olympic Stadium, the Elbphilharmonie in Hamburg, and the Perez Museum in Miami. Since 2006 they have been the architects for the multi-phased renovation and restoration of the Armory.

AI WEIWEI (China; works in Berlin). Renowned for making strong aesthetic statements that resonate with timely phenomena across today's geopolitical world. From architecture to installations, social media to documentaries, he uses a wide range of mediums as expressions of new ways for his audiences to examine society and its values.

Eleni Petaloti and Leonidas Trampoukis at the installation Athlos for the Art Athina, 2017. Ph. Matthieu Salvaing

Eleni Petaloti & Leonidas Trampoukis are LOT. Eleni Petaloti & Leonidas Trampoukis are objects of common interest.

LISA NAUDIN

It is fair to say that last year marked a turning point for these architects' careers. Both of their sibling practices—as they call them—took part in outstanding exhibitions in which they could deploy their aptitudes to shift from one scale to the other with subtle sophistication. The object within architecture, the architecture within the object, coexist in their mode of thought in the form of a reciprocal relation based in design, material, and production processes.

Petaloti and Trampoukis left their home country of Greece ten years ago to pursue their graduate studies at the University of Columbia and then chose to stay in New York. In 2012, after other work experiences and learning from their new environment, they founded the architectural and design firm LOT with offices in both Greece and New York. Three years later, the younger objects of common interest arrived to support the former, caring about details and the haptic nature of things. In their own words: "When working, they are united by a shared background, each other, and a passion for transforming the everyday. Common projects span scopes and domains; one's projects are sparked by the other's. An installation or an interior can result in an object, material experiments of furniture production find their way in architectural installations." They began designing objects randomly as an exercise, the purpose was not to design specific furniture for a particular project but to find a form of artistic exploration with physical models while figuring out the role they played in larger spaces.

Theirs is, then, a total design project with the aim to create objects, installations, and spaces in a way that opens up the possibility of investigating material and conceptual inspirational moments. Despite their interest in this wide range of scales, Petaloti and Trampoukis consider themselves to be architects more than designers. This is probably because their upmost interest is in the production processes. They highly value specialized craftsmanship, precedence, and know-hows. They look for producers that have maintained a strong commitment with making, even when exploring new materials and technologies.

One could say that there exists a poetic and even counterintuitive affiliation between these processes and the very abstract and pure family of forms that identify LOT's and objects of common interest's work. Blunt forms are sometimes cold and hard when being touched, and vice versa, promising the user some discovery and surprise, as well as turning their focus, again, to the haptic.

LOT also works on space and urban context. Sky-Line was a very visible public installation that intended to engage passersby in an intimate interaction within and around the space. It was first placed at the footsteps of Flatiron building and was shaped by tubular white arched components that defined and outlined a trapezoidal galleria: "Each of the arches is lit along its whole length, a smoothly transitioning lighting effect from daytime to nighttime, transforming the look and experience of the installation while making it highly visible from a distance and from above." Some white net hammocks were hanging from each of the arches, inviting the public to participate by playing, hanging out, gazing, socializing, or just resting in the magnificent surroundings of the Flatiron Plaza. The installation was the result of winning the First Prize of an invited competition organized by the Van Alen Institute.

Later, the installation was shipped and reinstalled under the cantilever structure of the Pierre Lassonde building, OMA's extension of the Beaux Arts Museum in Quebec, Montreal. It was disposed in a slightly different way to respond to its new context, provoking a new spatial experience.

Among their works, Project Jura (LOT) and Table of Contents (objects of common interest) can serve to summarize the sibling practices' different scale and material interests. The former was done in collaboration with KNOWSPACE as part of an invited workshop that set out to design a unique wilderness accommodation in the mountains of Jura, Switzerland. The pavilion consisted of an elevated and introverted ring structure in which the perimeter hosted the common areas, bathroom, and kitchen. The center worked as a middle-perforated net communal dormitory for up to eight people, thought of as a mattress that could be used to gaze and experience the forest. Table of Content is a pop-up restaurant concept for the Belgic Biennale INTERIEUR, in which the gastronomic and spatial experiences were designed as a 'calming force' where visitors can escape to. Some exuberant vegetation collaborated with a display of various marbles and food design to generate a communal, yet intimate, environment.

One of their latest projects is a branch shop in downtown Brooklyn for Devoción, the soon to be opened farm-to-table coffee roaster. The commission for this new space included a grand bar counter with a jungle island in the center. The design is inspired by the relationship between The United States and Colombia. Everything—from chairs to tiles and cabinets—are collaborative craftwork done between Bogotá and New York.

Most recently, Petaloti and Trampoukis participated at the Martinos Antique and Fine Art Gallery exhibition in Greece. It was an opportunity to introduce The Memory Chair and Table, two of their new objects that stand as the result of synthetic exercises based in the interaction of materials, colors, and transparency, articulation and contradiction of forms. This balance can be found in almost each piece designed by objects of common interest, including in the Marble Mirror, the Bent Stool, the Layer Stools or the Relativity of Color glassware series.

Last December, LOT and objects of common interest, in partnership with Maharam (maharam.com), were responsible for the Design Talks Theater at Design Miami/. Under the name, Spectacle, they designed a space that was unified by a continuous perimeter of amber arcade mirrors, which reflected actors and audience members generating a reverberating atmosphere. A variety of sitting furniture with a non-hierarchical arrangement invited the audience to actively participate in the debates.

Petaloti and Trampoukis use synthetic and mineral materials such as copper, marble, or glass, and push their limits in terms of forms and combinations. Like a tiny architecture work, every object is about aesthetics, structure, identity, transparency, light, and volume. Each fabrication process has a unique story to tell. Some prototypes have even been designed in New Jersey, made of local marble in Greece, and then assembled in The Netherlands.

Working constantly between two very different worlds is something that has made an impact on Petaloti and Trampoukis's design thinking. Greece is a much calmer environment than New York; each place has a particular sense of light, materiality, and volume. New York is a fast and proactive environment that constantly offers tons of stimulus and sources of inspiration. This duality of living, bouncing from one country to the other, presents demanding and perpetual challenges. In that sense, their work tends to be very precise but not contextual.

The sibling relationship between LOT and objects of common interest is defined by their creators as one in which "support is not a selfless act of affection, but a fostering of productive potential."

Sky–Line

PUBLIC INSTALLATION

SKY–LINE

DATE: 2017 / LOCATION: Pierre Lassonde Pavilion, Québec, Canada / CLIENT: Musée National des Beaux-Arts du Québec MNBAQ / STATUS: Built / DESIGN TEAM: Eleni Petaloti, Leonidas Trampoukis, Vincent Meyer Madaus, Isabel Sarasa Mené / COLLABORATORS: MAP Studio (Lighting Design), Daniel Urrutia for AUE structural engineers (Structural Engineers), FABRIC IMAGES Inc, Elgin, IL (Fabrication), 4th State Metals, New York (Installation) / PHOTOS: LOT, Vincent Meyer Madaus

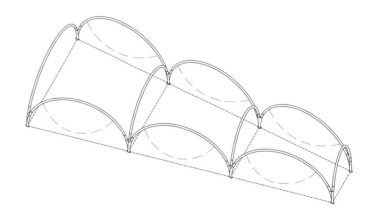

FLATIRON SKY–LINE

DATE: 2016 / LOCATION: Flatiron Plaza, 4th State Metals, New York, USA / CLIENT: Flatiron, 23rd Street Partnership, New York / STATUS: Built. Invited Competition by Van Alen Institute / DESIGN TEAM: Eleni Petaloti, Leonidas Trampoukis, Vincent Meyer Madaus / COLLABORATORS: MAP Studio (Lighting Design), Daniel Urrutia for AUE structural engineers (Structural Engineers), FABRIC IMAGES inc, Elgin, IL (Fabrication) / PHOTOS: Bryan W. Ferry

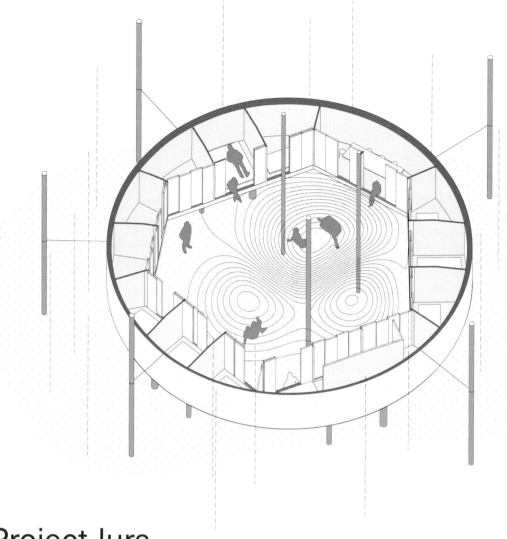

Project Jura

WILDERNESS ACCOMMODATION

DATE: 2015 / LOCATION: Saignelegier, Switzerland / SITE AREA: 5.6 m2 - 60 sf / CLIENT: Jura Tourism Office / STATUS: Competition entry, invited workshop by Jura Tourism office / DESIGN TEAM: Eleni Petaloti, Leonidas Trampoukis, Vincent Meyer Madaus, Isabel Sarasa Mené in collaboration with KNOWSPACE (Erhard An-He Kinzelbach) / IMAGES: Courtesy of LOT and objects of common interest

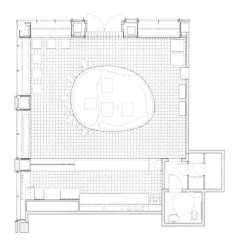

Devoción

COFFEE SHOP

DATE: 2017-2018 / LOCATION: Brooklyn, USA / SITE AREA: 50m2 - 538 sf / CLIENT: Devoción / STATUS: Under construction / DESIGN TEAM: Eleni Petaloti, Leonidas Trampoukis, Vincent Meyer Madaus, Isabel Sarasa Mené / IMAGES: Courtesy of LOT and objects of common interest

Table of Contents
POP-UP RESTAURANT CONCEPT

DATE: 2016 / LOCATION: Kortrijk, Belgium / STATUS: Competition entry, invited by Biennale INTERIEUR / DESIGN TEAM: Eleni Petaloti, Leonidas Trampoukis, Vincent Meyer Madaus, Isabel Sarasa Mené / IMAGES: Courtesy of LOT and objects of common interest

Memory Acts:
Memory Chair & Table

PUBLIC EXHIBITION

DATE: November 2017 / LOCATION: Martinos Palace, Athena, Greece / CLIENT: Martinos Antique and Fine Art Gallery / STATUS: Completed / DESIGN TEAM: Eleni Petaloti, Leonidas Trampoukis / MATERIAL: Steel, colored glass and marble / PHOTOS: Dimitris Kleanthis

Spectacle

DESIGN TALKS THEATER AT DESIGN MIAMI

DATE: October 2017 / LOCATION: Miami Beach, Florida, USA / CLIENT: Design Miami / STATUS: Built / DESIGN TEAM: Eleni Petaloti, Leonidas Trampoukis, Vincent Meyer Madaus, Isabel Sarasa Mené in partnership with Maharam / COLLABORATORS: Bolon, Roechling, Propylaea, AAMSCO, Technogel / PHOTOS: Brooke Holm

Objects of common interest: Relativity of Color, Marble Mirror, Bent Stool, and Side Table

Eleni Petaloti, Leonidas Trampoukis
PHOTOS: Brooke Holm

"The real architectural commodity is the collaboration, the featuring, the x. Support in the metaphysical manifested in the produced."

Lena Wimmer

Architects

This young German architect is developing a singular career in design, research, and teaching. She is an outside-the-box thinker whose projects include experiments in space infrastructure and floating columns.

DANIELA FREIBERG

Ph. Magnus Pettersson

In 2014, Lena Wimmer completed her Masters in Architecture at the Universität der Künste (UdK) in Berlin. During her time as a student she travelled, living in Milan and Rome, studying Architecture at the Academia di Brera and at the Berlage Institute in Rotterdam, and enjoying countless hours at the Columbia University Library. After graduating, she established Lena Wimmer Architects at her apartment in Berlin until she moved the office to its current location in the Kreuzberg district, in 2016. There, she leads a small team that works mainly on commissions. A shop window brings the neighborhood inside and lets the team share their work routine with curious pedestrians.

Beyond her work in design and building, Wimmer carries out research in various areas. "Encounter," an indepdendent research project to Outer Space, led her to delve into space architecture; in "Rebuilding Aleppo," she conducted field research in the Middle East, looking to define parameters for societies when there is high risk of civil war; in "New York Block 2085," another theoretical project, Wimmer proposes a new layer for the urban pattern, focusing on New York and rethinking the proposition of living in a high-rise.

Wimmer insists that her education has been guided by her interests and the depth with which she likes to take certain topics. And even though she is committed to her academic career—she is now a Visiting Professor at the Technische Universität (TU) in Berlin—she believes that formal education is as important as personal experience:"I have probably learned more outside the university, much

more." During her early youth, she never pictured herself studying architecture; she read literature, was interested in astronomy, and wondered about being an artist and 'universal scholar,' in the old-fashioned way as she herself describes it. Yet, she felt art was everywhere and could not be studied from one to six in the afternoon. She began to research writers, philosophers, and filmmakers she was interested in, and realized that many of them were originally trained as architects. It was in the field that she found the possibility of combining her diverse interests: science, humanities, nature ... and became fascinated.

We asked Wimmer about a dream commission she would like to have in the future. She eyed projects that work and that would last, thus giving feedback over the long term: "I hope I will work on projects that, in the end, create an environment."

FUTURE NEW YORK, ALEPPO AND SPACE INFRASTRUCTURE

Wimmer developed a futuristic New York as student in 2011. The project focuses on New York and is built from research into high-rise living, asking, how will the future be developed? How will a community live within a hybrid project? The High Rise concept is transformed into a horizontal skyscraper that rethinks the idea of floors and movements inside the block by lifting the traditional New York block with flying drones parking on top of the building.

Following her research on societies that are at risk and in conflicts over resources, a field she became involved with during a trip to Bolivia and Peru in 2007, Wimmer's work on Aleppo examined a society with a high risk of civil war. Her interest began when she first arrived after a long motorbike trip from Rome. The largest Syrian city before the civil war, Aleppo, had undergone considerable destruction and damage, particularly since 2012, when the armed conflict reached the city. "Rebuilding Aleppo" is a project she has been involved with since 2015 as founding member of "Strategies to Rebuild Aleppo." Together with a group of European architects and scientists from the Middle East, a Manifest details strategies to rebuild the city, including short and long term goals, and short and medium term activities with the inhabitants. The work also involves an examination and critique of visions for Aleppo's future.

"Encounter" is Wimmer's most recent research project. She began it before finishing her degree in 2013 and expects to publish it in 2018. "Mankind can be characterized by an eternal drive to overcome the impossible, to make the unknown known," she says. "Encounter" is an independent research project conducted in collaboration with NASA, ESA, Roscosmos,[1] UdK in Berlin, ETH Zürich (Eidgenössische Technische Hochschule) and TU Dresden (Technische Universität). The project is a contribution to future encounters: an infrastructure network system developed for outer space. The proposal reminded us of "L'Architettura interplanetaria" (Interplanetary Architecture - 1972), a film by the radical Italian architecture group Superstudio, which imagined similar structures, including a highway from the earth to the moon.[2] However, projects considered utopias or experimental decades ago—they spiked in number after 1969 moon landing—are seemingly more and more feasible today, and Wimmer proposes that they suggest new plausible conditions for life.

Besides doing the desktop research, Wimmer met with the men and women working to realize the dream of encounter: scientists in their laboratories, at universities, in companies, in governmental institutions, studios, and offices, and her research includes 30 interviews that encouraged, reinforced, and substantiated her proposed scenario. Discussing the premise of her project with astronauts, mission analysts, scientists and teachers of future astronauts, enabled her to prepare seven case studies for interventions in the solar system. Nano-scientists spoke of ongoing developments in materials for extreme environments and self-constructing hybrids, and plants manipulated by biotechnologists to live both on earth and in spaceships. Here, Earth is the starting point of an infrastructure network.

Her question, "What can be learned from past efforts to develop knowledge for the future?" led her to speak with historians, philosophers, and architects.

Wimmer's proposal includes seven exemplary stations made up of infrastructural stops on asteroids, moons, and minor planets like Eros, Phobos, Vesta, Ida, Titan, Pholus, and Halley, and which will operate as a case study to enable future journeys and missions to new territories. These stations act as nodal points of the solar network map, between Earth, Mars, Jupiter, Saturn, and Pluto. They are projected to provide different facilities and resources for travelers, like water, iron, gold, rare earth compounds, silicates, oxygen, food, and artificial gravity.

The station's chapters are organized into three parts. The first is a collection of state-of-the-art known facts about the building site. The second illustrates future plans for organizations and private firms on the site. The third could be described as a 'contemporary fairytale': an imaginary scenario for the site-specific stationary project. A self-regulating machine in a native, un-exploited soil narrates everyday life, describing the tenants, transients, and guest's routine. The book is built around thousands of known planets, moons, and asteroids that can be imagined as sites for future encounters.

Lena Wimmer's work draws from her personal story. Her interest in space has a particularly outstanding precedent: her grandmother, Helga Wimmer was a trained astronaut in the seventies and among the first women selected for a space shuttle mission, launched to conduct experiments. Thus, Wimmer's pursuit to find a route from Earth to Mars, has family roots.

We were taken by our conversation with this enthusiastic young architect, who immediately transmits warmth while reflecting her determined commitment to her diverse work.

1   NASA, United States National Aeronautics and Space Administration. ESA, European Space Agency. The Roscosmos State Corporation for Space Activities of the Russian Federation.

2   Founded in December 1966 by Adolfo Natalini and Cristiano Toraldo di Francia, later joined by Gian Piero Frassinelli, Roberto and Alessandro Magris, and Alessandro Poli, Superstudio was one of the most influential groups of the world avant-garde scene during the sixties and seventies.

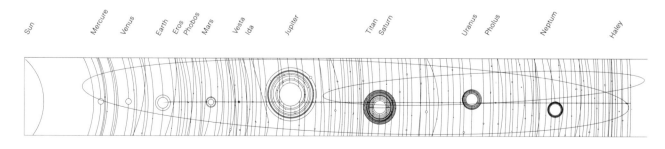

Proposal to make a road through the solar system by implementing infrastructural stops on certain asteroids moons and minor planets like Eros, Phobos, Vesta, Ida, Titan, Pholus, and Halley as seven proposed stops.

Burning Man

INSTALLATION AND LIVING SPACES

DATE: 2017 - 2018 / LOCATION: Gate Road, Black Rock City, Nevada, United States / SITE AREA: 300,000 m2 – 3,229,173.13 sf / INSTALLATION AREA: 15,000 m2 – 161,458.66 sf / CLIENT: Burning man Festival - Sebastian Sauvé / STATUS: to be built 2018 / DESIGN TEAM: Lena Wimmer, Sebastian Gubernatis, Lea Kruger

A New Yorker involved in the organization of Burning Man who had visited and loved Anomalie in Berlin, wanted to meet the architect in charge. He met Lena Wimmer, invited her to work on a proposal, and after seeing the idea, immediately started to work on it. The project has already been contracted for the festival's 2018 edition.

The installation consists of a set of floating elements with dimensions that can be changed, but are proposed as 24 x 6 feet and between 40 to 70 feet tall. The elements are 'flying curtains' shaped as silver columns and operated by programmed drones.

It takes only a few seconds to get them up in or out of the air. A weather-reading hardware on one drone connects with the others, as well as with Burning Man organization and the airport. A program will be used to direct each one and synchronize their positions, shaping alternative plans.

Wimmer worked very closely with the European drone company, and they are now developing their own software and hardware for the Burning Man project, which includes 36 drones: two, three and four drones per column, depending on each case.

The material that makes up the main columns was sewed in Berlin and is made from a combination of silver and golden fabric used for satellite isolation. Includes four nylon layers which provide necessary resistance—as it is a material that tolerates both high and low temperatures.

A complete prototype was made in Berlin to serve as a model for the fabrication in the United States. Lena Wimmer's team will travel to mount the installation in time for the festival's opening.

Burning Man Festival has taken place annually since 1986 in the Black Rock Desert of Nevada. Tens of thousands of people gather to celebrate and participate in the effort to co-create Black Rock City, a temporary metropolis dedicated to community, art, self-expression, and self-reliance. Burning Man defines itself as an atypical festival; it is, rather, a city wherein almost everything that happens is created entirely by its citizens, who are active participants in the experience.

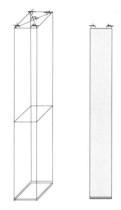

Variations of endless possibilities to arrange the columns.

Construction concept: 24 flying curtain columns.

Ph. Magnus Pettersson

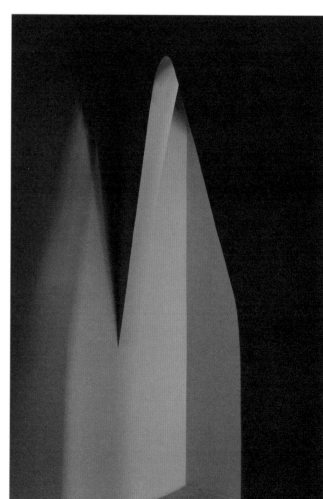

Anomalie Art Club

DATE: 2014 - 2017 / LOCATION: Prenzlauerberg, Berlin / SITE AREA: 2,000 m2 – 21,500 sf / BUILT AREA: 1,000 m2 – 10,800 sf / CLIENT: Jeremy & Jesse Carayol Ajwani s.f.k. / STATUS: built / DESIGN TEAM: Lena Wimmer / COLLABORATORS: Engineering: Timm Hofmeister. Fire proof systems: Eng. Maedebach-Redelik. Sound Acoustic: Stereo Studioservice Sven Roehrig. Contractor: Jarek Jakubil GmbH. Investor: Cosimo Gol

Anomalie is a French, family-run gallery, bar, restaurant, and club, located in Prenzlauerberg, Berlin. The collaboration began nine years ago in Milan, when the clients decided to create a new concept in Germany. Years later, a unique property appeared, an ideal space to house the concept—a fifties car garage in central Berlin. Lena Wimmer was granted utmost freedom to work on the design. It was a relationship based on a lot of trust, she admits: "We immediately wanted to challenge this place, transforming it into a science fiction cathedral that could be on Mars, but somehow landed in Berlin." The space looked to give the city a forum for music, art, culture, and high quality food from a French chef with one of the first Michelin stars awarded to his local green kitchen. Anomalie is located in the center of Berlin, near Mitte, Alexandre Platz and Dominique Perrault's Olympic Stadium, in a mix-use, very transited area that faces a slow transformation, and is made up of different facilities, apart housing, small shops, craftsmen, and entrepreneurs. Wimmer is attracted to these non-places, where a particular rhythm, lacking perfection, still maintains a feeling that one can encounter freedom.

The building would be hidden if not for an entrance that grabs attention, sticking out of the construction while the interior stays hidden from the observer.

Upon entering through the six-meter-high sliding door, the visitor unconsciously feels the outside noise disappear while being led by bent walls into the building. Shimmering grays on the walls and floors hold up a purple-red ceiling that bathes him in warm light. From here, the visitor is in-between different openings, curves, and doors that lead to the restaurant, club, gallery, and bar.

The building utilized simple construction and material techniques to complete the project on a tight budget, thereby saving money for some great handcrafted details. The decision complemented the luxury already present: a new shaking body was placed into a construction with six-meter-high ceilings, concrete columns, and an old glass façade. High chimney windows top the ceiling to let in a natural light that enters the inner core obliquely, through the translucent glass doors.

With round corners, no ninety degree angles, parabolic openings, and doors, one enters a space that is strange, but quiet and simple, at the same time.

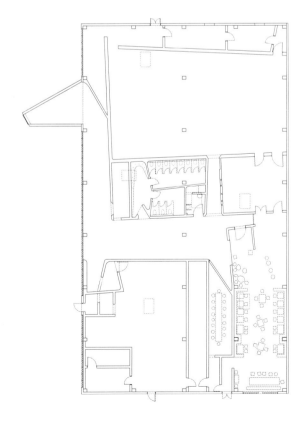

Plan

The name and concept were born out of the desire to deviate from the norm, the rule, from its rigidities and continuous subliminal suggestions, while underlining the ever-new righteousness of being oneself—as individuals, and as a collective. Anomalie does not need to follow any trends, patterns, or systems, it falls out of them, while creating a deviance, a novelty, a variation. Since its opening to the public, the space hosts three thousand people each weekend, with a thousand more in the garden. It is also used for events held by international brands and was chosen as a venue for Berlin Fashion Week.

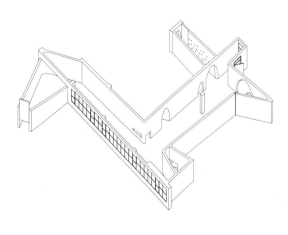

Axonometric

"We immediately wanted to challenge this place, transforming it into a science fiction cathedral that could be on Mars, but somehow landed in Berlin." LW

Anna W. von Huber writes about Anomalie

"The building adapts unconditionally
to its surroundings."

Architecture is both a method of building and the art of opening a dialogue between a construction and its surroundings, linking perception, adaptation, and connections. The young architect Lena Wimmer, in her design for the cultural site Anomalie, offers an interesting and versatile building. Anomalie is an attempt to minimally intervene in an existing structure through a kind of modification which is not consciously perceived, but rather appears subconsciously and quietly behind the mirror of shadow. The observer and visitor are drawn into the interior life of the building. In that process, the spirit, without exertion, follows the interior structure, which is primarily expressed in high walls and the play of light and shade. The interior structure is not intended to generate obvious presentations, but to subconsciously guide. The future combines with the present, and technology serves as a tool for development. Everything and nothing becomes the focus of events. It is an architecture that does not reveal itself through particularly pronounced signs and symbols, but which subtly adapts to its environment and thereby makes its own mark, such as the highly individual form of the interior doors or the crooked window as a reception area.

The visitor is guided by the architecture. Lena Wimmer creates a form of architecture which is publicly accessible, which neither explains nor offers explanations, but rather guides the subconscious. This architecture, or its thought-process, follows the principle of an interior order of humanity which is logical in itself (cf. Carl Gustav Jung). This interior order can symbolize the subconscious of the person, which cannot be observed in the deliberate perception and contemplation of external influences, but only shows itself to be accessible.

This access is not to be explicable, but experiential—open to experience through the spheres of human sensation, such as hearing, sight, and touch. In order to approach this building, a person will need, not pure reason, but intuition. This mental starting-point makes it possible to create a building which can be experienced on the one condition of human perception. It requires no foreknowledge of any intellectual surface.

The principle of color plays its own part in her architecture. Color becomes subordinate to shade. Light and shade are the elements used in this building. The light stands for change; like shade, it changes. Shade is a necessity in architecture.

A light kind of shade: close to the mightiest of people, almost regularly, as if it were bound to them, there is a soul of light. It is, as it were, the shadow that those cast.[1]

A link can be found with Tanizaki Jun'ichiro's essay "In praise of shadows."[2] Jun'ichiro follows Japanese naturalism and the theory that truth cannot be explained, but must be experienced. William James[3] or Friedrich Nietzsche represent parallels in Western thought. Wimmer's architecture does not explain, but is experienced. At the same time, one has, as a visitor, a feeling of immediate closeness, of a certain naturalness, which is evident on the one hand in this minimalist use of color, but also in the very detailed and muted arrangement of doors and walls. The only use of color is in the use of crimson. This element shows another important and recurring feature of this architecture, the power of nature.

"And should nature, ever true to itself, not have pointed us to the medium in which all the powers of creation work? In the deepest abysses of becoming, where we see nascent life, we become aware of the undiscovered and thus functioning element that we call by the inadequate name

light, ether, life-warmth, and that may be the sensory apparatus of the All-creating, with which He animates and warms all."[4] Crimson is the color of the embryo. The sinks show the power of water. Water is to represent a power and to evoke a sensibility for the elements of nature. The walls of the restrooms are raised very high and the sinks are set low in order to particularly emphasize the power of nature.

Looking at Anomalie in this way, it is not the large, notable features, such as plainly obtruding colors or scale, doors, or materials, but rather the many subtle features that change something in the mind and perception of the visitor. The reception is an example. The crooked window is not simply crooked, but set so low that the heads of the staff cannot be seen. Something is going on here...

"Art is being surprised at being surprised again and again by the same work of art, by discovering new things, by being drawn from one's world into the world of another, by entering into dialogue."

1   Friedrich, Nietzsche. "The Wanderer and His Shadow," 1880.

2   Jun'ichirō, Tanizaki. "In praise of shadows," 1933.

3   William, James. "The meaning of truth: a sequel to 'Pragmatism'," 1909.

4   Johann Gottfried, Herder. "Reflections on the philosophy of the history of mankind," 1784.

Anna W von Huber is a German philosopher and writer. She has published articles in several printed and online magazines. Her work specializes in Nietzsche, Kant, and contemporary French philosophers, like Valery, Lyotard and Hölderlin. She holds broader interests in philosophy, art, music, and architecture.

Report—ness:
Detroit

Timeline and Infographics:
Lisa Naudin and Mariam Samur

Visual essays:
Pablo Gerson

In his curatorial text for the Shrinking Cities[1] conference in 2004, Kyong Park used Detroit as the main case study for the phenomenon, and concluded with one open question: do shrinking cities grant greater power to global capitalism, or are they the places where post-capitalist economic models will form?

Fourteen years later, the picture has become even more complex; and still is quite blurry. The emergence of the sharing economies, as well as other alternative models, have impacted our societies to the point that we need to rethink and redefine all of our terminology. The global political landscape that has taken shape over the last few years offers another reaction to these changes. We are witnessing how conservativism, extremism, and various forms of fanaticism flourish in times of uncertainty.

Detroit represents the climax and decay of a global project that was encapsulated in the

American Dream—of progress related to a heroic industrialization, of welfare related to consumerism, of economic growth related to urban sprawl, of social integration. The Motor City's streets lewdly show the physical trials and scars of the 20th century, that seem to be claiming to be re-signified. The city that was once the cradle of Fordism and experiments in production found itself ahead of the curve in another kind of process in which there was a shrinking timetable of change. It all happened so rapidly that the demand for adaptation was overwhelming for everybody and everything.

Today we face the peculiar results of those urban processes; here, a recession is not the same as a reversal, as returning back in time. Decentralization, dispersion and communication have supplanted infrastructure, a densifying fabric, and physical exchange of capital. Since Google replaced Ford, the rural and the urban are no longer opposites. Detroit's coexistent singularity and commonality

have inspired new ways of thinking about the contemporary city and its problematics—Charles Waldheim's concept of Landscape Urbanism[2] was, for instance, inspired by these processes. Over the last few decades, this critical territory and its social complexity have also required the testing of new models and fostered needed innovations, startups, and entrepreneurship. There is no clear map for ideal progress, there is no certain light at the end of the tunnel.

In this report, we bring together a historical analysis by Lisa Ubelaker Andrade, interviews with Maurice Cox (Director of Planning and Development Department) and Steven Lewis (Design Director of the Central Region) to learn about the present and speculate about the future of Detroit, we feature some proposals and projects for the city, and we draw a portrait of it through our own curious and questioning lenses.

The Motor City is now an un-patterned laboratory.

FLORENCIA RODRIGUEZ

1.   Kyong Park, "Shrinking City Detroit," in: "Working paper: Complete Works 1 – Detroit," available online at: shrinking cities/fileadmin/shrink/downloads/pdfs/III_1_Studies1
2.   Charles Waldheim, "Landscape as Urbanism: A General Theory," Princeton: Princeton University Press, 2016.

For a casual observer, one who blithely follows the news, the mere mention of the city of Detroit evokes images of a post-industrial landscape. Detroit, the familiar story goes, was the backbone of the U.S. industrial age, the home to the nascent automobile industry, and the celebrated 'arsenal of democracy' during World War II. Fifty years later, the city was the graveyard of a declining industrial era, a symbol of urban crisis. Indeed, over the last several years, the national and international press has taken interest in the tragic fate of the Motor City. While some detail the deteriorated landscape and illustrate its fall from grace with photographs of a seemingly deserted city, others have suggested it to be a space uniquely poised for reinvention and open to new investments.

LISA UBELAKER ANDRADE

Reinvention and Resoluteness: A Brief History of Detroit

Yet, as historians like Thomas Sugrue and Beth Tompkins Bates[1] have shown, the experience of crisis in Detroit has been, and continues to be, more complex than the simplistic narratives of industrial decline and burgeoning investment often allow us to believe. Terms like 'revitalization' and 'urban renewal' have complex and controversial pasts. Certainly, Detroit is a city that has lived many lives, that has been reformulated and recreated by the people and the industries that it has housed. It is, likewise, a city that has endured considerable strife, tensions, and dire inequalities, among its residents and at the hand of problematic policies. These experiences color the city's past as much as its future, provoking ongoing questions about the moral, economic, cultural, and racial ramifications of present-day decisions. At the same time, they also underline that the singular constant in Detroit's history has been a powerful, and sometimes painful, state of reinvention.

Even before Detroit was Detroit, it was an area of land that seemed to perpetually change hands. The frontier town, once home to a number of indigenous tribes, became a French settlement in 1701, was taken over by the British after the French and Indian War, won to the United States in the American Revolution, and briefly retrieved by the British in 1812, only to be re-incorporated into U.S. territory shortly thereafter. By the beginning of the 19th century, it was a city that would be defined by both its diversity and its spirit of resilience. When the city caught fire in June 1805, it was nearly completely destroyed. As residents worked to rebuild and develop a new, more modern urban plan, the idea of renewal became emblazoned on the city flag: "*Speramus meliora; resurgent cineribus*," reads the city's prophetic motto: "We hope for better things; it shall arise from the ashes."

So it did. Detroit grew in size and in stature in the 19th century, becoming a hub for European immigrants, as well as commercial entrepreneurs and industrialists who reaped the benefits of the Gilded Age. The new rich of Detroit built Victorian mansions along East Jefferson, many of which still stand today. By the Civil War, a small but important Black community grew in size. Detroit's proximity to Canada, where slavery was illegal since 1834, made the city a significant stop on the Underground Railroad. Yet, despite its location in a free territory, Detroit saw entrenched tensions grow between its European immigrant and Black residents during the war. Dailies like the "Detroit Free Press" stoked immigrant communities to view Black residents as competition for jobs, and suggested that the end of slavery would garner labor competition from free Blacks. German and Irish Catholics rioted in protest of a draft into the Union Army in 1863, marking the first in what would be a long line of racially-driven conflicts.

It was not until the 20th century that Detroit would truly grow in size and stature, not only rising rapidly in terms of population, but garnering a special status in the American imagination. In 1896, Henry Ford constructed his first automobile in Detroit, and after a few false starts, in 1903, he began the company that would change the landscape of the city. Ford's cars and their style of manufacturing introduced several innovations to both U.S. industry and consumer culture: his Model T automobile, manufactured in Highland Park, was built using a moving assembly line, a style of production that transformed the industry by boosting output, economiz-

1   Thomas Sugrue. "The Origins of the Urban Crisis: Race and Inequality in Postwar Detroit." Updated Edition. Princeton University Press, 2014; Beth Tompkins Bates. "The Making of Black Detroit in the Ages of Henry Ford." Chapel Hill: University of North Carolina Press, 2012.

ing production, and cementing Detroit's future as the new hub of the automobile industry. Model Ts could be quickly produced at accessible prices.

The labor conditions of the assembly line, however, were quite grueling—turnover was high and competition with other factories, like General Motors, also in Detroit, quickly generated challenges for the company. Thus, it was not until Ford put in place another business innovation that Detroit became a mythologized destination for those in search of the American Dream. In a move that bypassed union negotiations and put emphasis on production and the bottom line, Ford doubled the pay of laborers to five dollars per day and vastly improved conditions of contract. The factory work was still taxing, but working at Ford meant an eight hour work day and a forty hour work week—luxuries in a pre-labor legislation era. Production skyrocketed and consumer spending grew.

News of the famous $5 work day spread quickly. Migrants and immigrants poured into the city. As a result, Detroit's racial and cultural diversity likewise blossomed. The city's population grew from a mere 265,000, in 1900, to more than 1.5 million by 1930. The vast majority of laborers were white migrants and immigrants from Europe, but Ford and other Detroit companies also became famous for hiring Black workers, though they were hired often for more menial positions and in segregated stations. Ford's particularly esteemed reputation in the Black community, Thompkins Bates reminds us, was largely due to the number of jobs open to Black workers and its pay, rather than the quality of those positions or potential for promotion. Nevertheless, the opportunity meant that Detroit would become a destination during the Great Migration, when thousands of Black men and women left the South in search of improved opportunities in

the northern industrial cities. The population particularly boomed during World War I, when immigration stalled and new opportunities for work opened up for people of color. The Black population in Detroit rose from 5,800 African Americans in 1910 to nearly 41,000 in 1920—a number that would continue to grow over the following years.

Growth in numbers, however, did not necessarily mean that Detroit's neighborhoods became more diverse or equitable. The city's geography was racially divided. Black Bottom, named for the richness of its soil, was located on the city's East Side and was home to most of the city's Black residents. Racist policies confined Black migrants to the area. Hastings Street, a hub for Black businesses, became a lively epicenter of Black culture. In housing, labor, law enforcement, education, and daily life, racism was a powerful and everyday reality for the growing community.

At the same time, the competitive pay, powerful unions, and the expansion of the automobile industry in the twenties, made the auto industry, for whites in particular, a place for socioeconomic mobility: it spurred consumer culture, making the laborers themselves able to afford the products they produced. Vast middle and professional classes also developed. The city's landscape mimicked these changes, and the skyline showed signs of the wealth that arrived via the automobile industry. A few new modern apartment buildings were built in the twenties and the city celebrated the construction of new skyscrapers, like the Landmark Guardian Building and the Fisher Building, downtown. Bustling shopping districts served a growing consumer base. Among these were the flagship J. L. Hudson Department Store: Hudson's, as it was known, boasted a massive floor space that was only rivaled by Macy's in New York. It became an icon of the mid-century Detroit experience. Notably, its expansion to the suburbs in 1954, the building's closure and 1983 and subsequent demolition in 1998, likewise serve as popular markers of downtown decline.

As one might expect, the depression hit Detroit's economy hard. Production faltered and declined in the thirties; but again, the city revived. Unions, strengthened in the thirties, mobilized and achieved important gains for auto industry workers. By 1940, just prior to official U.S. entry into World War II, the city went back to work: the auto plants were quickly converted into armament factories, and residents—men and women—were trained to build tanks, military hardware, and planes. Detroit expanded as the 'arsenal of democracy.' Unemployment plummeted. At the same time, however, racism simmered. Even while the Black community benefited from new wartime employment opportunities, several New Deal policies were driving up inequalities and reinforcing a racist urban structure. Among these was the practice of redlining. In 1934, the Federal Housing Authority

was formally established and with it, a number of policies were put in place that sought to generate growth by offering investments in homeownership. The policies also, however, rated neighborhoods as areas of investment; due to their poor ratings, Black neighborhoods like Black Bottom were 'red-lined,' they were excluded from development and, moreover, white neighborhoods were further incentivized to exclude Black residents from moving in. With investments in Black neighborhoods halted, conditions worsened: the single family homes that so typically dominated the landscape were becoming overcrowded, converted into apartments, all while still lacking some basic services.

As the housing shortage continued and Black laborers made more headway in the defense industry, conflict erupted. In 1941, Detroit broke ground on two sets of public housing buildings intended to provide relief for the housing shortage: one was intended to be for white laborers, and a second, the Sojourner Truth Housing project, for Black residents. As both were located in predominantly Polish neighborhoods, white residents protested, mobilizing in opposition of Black housing outside of a Black neighborhood. Klu Klux Klan members rallied around the issue, intimidating Black families from moving into buildings. Several Black families moved in despite the violence. Segregation practices continued as did racial tensions, which again erupted into violence in 1943, during a more prolonged episode of conflict. Meanwhile, the city continued to appear to herald a new era of production, churning out tanks, airplanes, and equipment for the war effort.

When the city turned back to automobiles in the postwar era, there were new engines driving the city's production: a prosperous postwar American economy that invited new innovations and a car-crazed culture bolstered by federal initiatives to build up the U.S. highway system. The social, economic and cultural impact of highway build-up across the United States was pro-

nounced, and in Detroit, the effects reverberated into almost every aspect of urban life. For one, highway construction offered an important boost to the automobile industry; the growth of suburbs and commuter culture required middle class families to double their car ownership. At the same time, construction also opened up new spaces, outside the city limits, for factories and affordable new homes. Detroit itself, then, became forever changed. Hudson's—the emblematic department store downtown—opened up a new shopping center outside the city limits in 1954. Factories also moved, building new facilities along the highway. And, of course, many of Detroit's residents followed. New suburban developments offered more space outside the city. The Detroit suburbs became a picture of the American Dream.

But it was a dream inaccessible to some. The repercussions of this era of suburbanization were manyfold, and the causes and nature of 'white flight' were not merely a question of a changing lifestyle. While 1954-1956 signal the beginning of the era of suburbanization, they also mark the first years in which the Supreme Court decision, Brown vs Board of Education, which deemed racial segregation in U.S. schools unconstitutional, was enforced in U.S. schools. In the several years following the decision, cities and towns across the country were forced to integrate their schooling systems. In light of this new mandate, white flight out of American cities did not only imply a movement to larger houses with two car garages, but also a new form of de facto segregation. The new suburban neighborhoods put in place policies to exclude Black homeownership. While some white suburbanites were explicit about their desire for exclusively white communities, others posed segregation in economic terms, convinced that integrated communities would drive down property values and endanger the post-war prosperity. Middle class Black families, desiring to move beyond the lower-quality housing in the city's deteriorating Black neighborhoods, found perpetual roadblocks and discrimination.

Suburbanization and highway construction also came with new initiatives at 'urban renewal' that largely targeted the severely declined Black Bottom neighborhood. The famed Hastings Street, a center of Black community, was demolished. Black Bottom was controversially razed, leaving it undeveloped for years, and turning portions over to highway development. Low-income residents were moved to housing projects elsewhere in the city. New developments, built in the sixties, sought to keep the city's middle classes from exiting the city, but white flight continued for the following decades, with the white population declining to 55% by 1970 and a mere 34% in 1980. Though some cite the violent 1967 riots as inciting the final exodus of white Detroiters, others note that other factors, including a failed mandate to desegregate the Detroit metropolitan area's schools, played a formidable role. The exodus also meant that tax revenue continued to plummet, and in turn, city revenue for the maintenance of public structures and development declined. Even Motown, the famed record label that bore the city's name and its legacy, picked up and moved to Los Angeles.

The downwind in the local economy was only hastened by a broader process of deindustrialization in the U.S. auto industry, and made more severe by rising crime, unemployment and poverty. An epidemic of crack addiction, corruption, and a rise in gang violence further damaged local communities and also stigmatized residents. In the 2000s, crime declined, but more prosperous economic times did not return. In the wake of the foreclosure crisis in 2008, Detroit property values hit rock bottom and its population continued to sink in numbers.

The city, deep in debt, fell under the control of the state, and then formally filed for bankruptcy in 2013. Many who had found the means to leave, had left; by the early twenty-tens, the city's population had dwindled to 700,000. Vacant lots peppered the landscape, boarded up homes and buildings made national news. It was, in many ways, a city abandoned—but there were also residents and communities, mostly Black, who remained and continued to call Detroit home.

'Those who stayed' continued to work to rebuild neighborhoods while fighting pervasive unemployment. They also began to see the signs of new interest in the city in the wake of bankruptcy. Just after word of $1 properties became national news, new investments began to appear. Quicken Loans owner Dan Gilbert poured a billion dollars into the city's downtown revitalization. Shortly thereafter, a number of speculative investors began to buy up the city's foreclosed properties for cheap, renovating homes, and making improvements. Although the speculative buying and signs of development were seen as positive for some, for others it raised important questions and potential costs. For example, the buy-up drove up property taxes and pushed many long time residents, unable to afford the new costs, into foreclosure. As a result, outside investors have bought up foreclosed homes, and are now charging rent to former owners and inhabitants.

Some also argue that the revitalization efforts appear disconnected from the problems facing the community. When a Whole Foods Market, a high priced organic supermarket chain, opened in the city's Inglewood neighborhood and tech industries were rumored to be surveying sites to set up shop downtown, lower income residents and community activists questioned whether 'revitalization' would keep existing communities' problems in mind, or be built solely to attract outsiders and generate profits for investors. Those who could remember the city's recent past could see in the promises of 'renewal' the troubling signs of gentrification. They

questioned if the new age of reforms would once again leave Detroit's Black communities outside of the circle of prosperity, and, as a result, threaten the few Black-owned businesses that had resolutely survived.

These voices have not gone completely unheard. New efforts by local community organizations, activists, and city government have approached Detroit's 'return' with a more concerted eye for community-based solutions. Detroit's Mayor, Mike Duggan, has been a key player: he has used his podium to speak directly about the history of redlining and the damage that has been done to Black communities, in particular, over the last several decades. He also set up policy plans that speak to concerns about inclusivity and displacement: residential developers that accept government tax incentives, for example, are being required to make 20% of their housing units 'affordable,' thus encouraging mixed-income spaces. This new framework is being hailed as innovative and connected by some; but others still see the new developments on the horizon as set to undercut local ownership, in favor of outsider wealth. Indeed, for many of those aware of the city's past, questions remain—as to how, for whom, and under what terms Detroit's latest reinvention will take place.

Planning History of Detroit

USA
CANADA
1

3

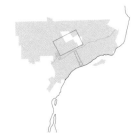
5

2

4

6

— Ribbon Farms
— Park Lots / U.S. Public Land Survey System
— Ten Thousand Acre Grid
○ Woodward plan
• Fort Pontchartrain

▬ Redevelopment projects
▬ Conservation projects

1. DETROIT FORTIFICATION
   & AGRICULTURAL FABRIC
   By 1730, Detroit developed its agriculture along the riverfront. The "ribbon farm" lots are long and narrow so that each could have access to the water. Several of the "ribbon farm" owners gave their names to the actual streets. The topology of the "Fort Pontchartrain du Detroit, 1764" drew the principal avenues of the actual Detroit.

2. AUGUSTUS B. WOODWARD PLAN
   & "TEN TOUSAND ACRE GRID"
   After the Great Fire of 1805, the governor decided to call Territorial Judge Augustus B. Woodward to develop a new urban fabric. In 1818, the plan was abandoned and only a fragment was used, that section is today's Downtown Detroit.

3. DETROIT IN 1825

4. JEFFERSON GRID WITH THE PRINCIPAL AVENUES
   The Jefferson Grid, developed by the U.S. Public Land Survey System, is a grid system used to implement propriety. It determines the orientation of the future of the urban fabric.

5. HIGH WAY AND RAIL SYSTEM
   The railroad system is an antecedent of the grid that led to contemporary morphology of Detroit. It could be said that the rail system was incorporated into the grid.

6. URBAN RENEWAL PROJECTS OF 1963
   Projects led by the Detroit City Plan Comission

Housing

Housing Type
92% Detroit's housing stock was built before 1980.
73% of the city housing is made of single-family house which define Detroit city housing structure.

Home Ownership

○ Owner-occupied
● Renter-occupied

365,528 Housing units - Vacancy rate

○ 255,740 occupied
● 109,788 vacant/abandoned structure

SOURCES:
June Manning Thomas and Henco Bekkering. "Mapping Detroit. Land, Community, and Shaping a City." Detroit: Wayne State University Press, 2015. pp.27-51.
Detroit Public Schools. Dept. of Social Studies. "Detroit: A Manual for Citizens." Detroit: Board of Education of the City of Detroit, Michigan University, 1958.
William L. Clements Library, University of Michigan. Map Division. Available online: clements/umich/maps

Public Lands Plan: Vacant Land

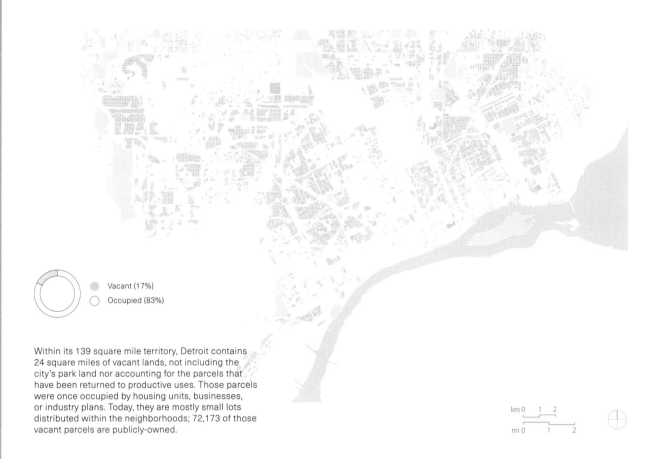

○ Vacant (17%)
○ Occupied (83%)

Within its 139 square mile territory, Detroit contains 24 square miles of vacant lands, not including the city's park land nor accounting for the parcels that have been returned to productive uses. Those parcels were once occupied by housing units, businesses, or industry plans. Today, they are mostly small lots distributed within the neighborhoods; 72,173 of those vacant parcels are publicly-owned.

km 0   1   2
mi 0   1   2

Ethnicity

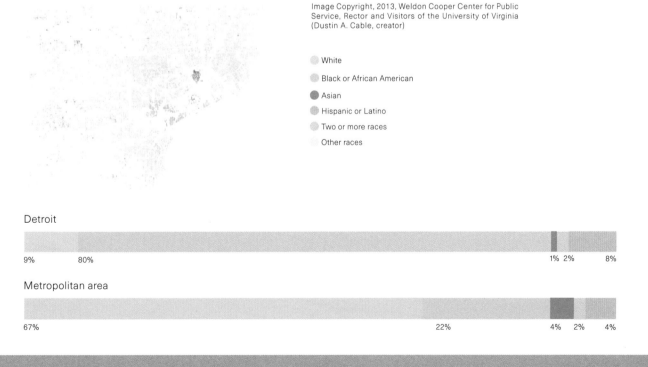

Image Copyright, 2013, Weldon Cooper Center for Public Service, Rector and Visitors of the University of Virginia (Dustin A. Cable, creator)

○ White
○ Black or African American
● Asian
○ Hispanic or Latino
○ Two or more races
○ Other races

Detroit

9%   80%   1% 2%   8%

Metropolitan area

67%   22%   4% 2%   4%

SOURCES:
"Public Lands Plan: Vacant Land" by Ted Schulzt, General & Strategic Planning, Planning and Development Department of the City of Detroit.
Extended by: Detroit Future City. Publications Special Reports in site of Detroit Future City. Available online: detroit future city/research
United States Census Bureau. Available online: census.gov/topics/population
Detroitography. Featuring and Creating Great Maps of Detroit. Available online: DETROITography

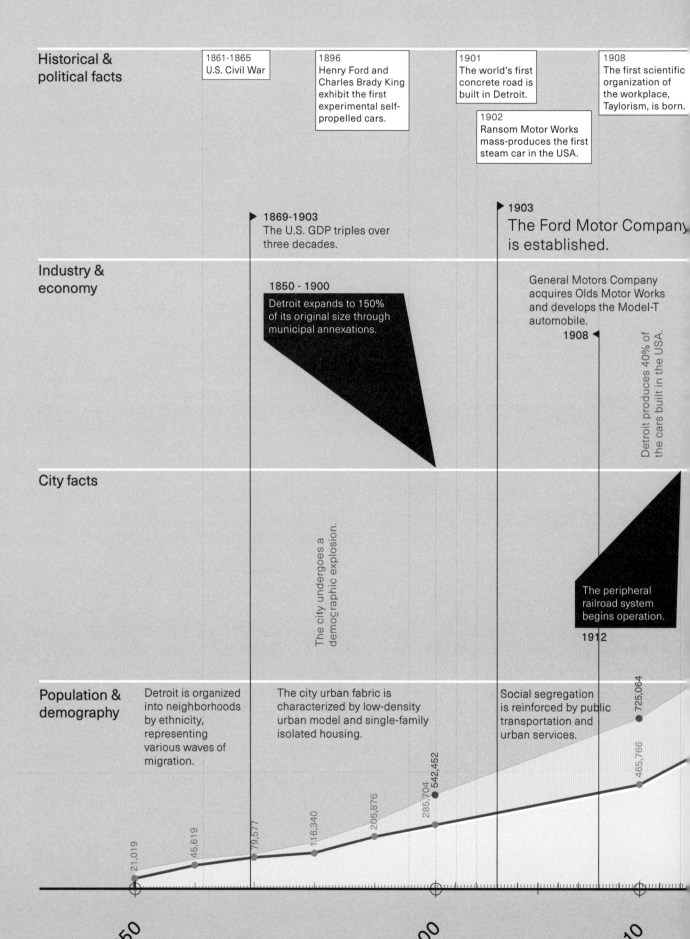

1875   1905   1912

Historical & political facts

1861-1865
U.S. Civil War

1896
Henry Ford and Charles Brady King exhibit the first experimental self-propelled cars.

1901
The world's first concrete road is built in Detroit.

1902
Ransom Motor Works mass-produces the first steam car in the USA.

1908
The first scientific organization of the workplace, Taylorism, is born.

▶ **1869-1903**
The U.S. GDP triples over three decades.

▶ **1903**
The Ford Motor Company is established.

Industry & economy

1850 - 1900
Detroit expands to 150% of its original size through municipal annexations.

General Motors Company acquires Olds Motor Works and develops the Model-T automobile.
1908 ◀

Detroit produces 40% of the cars built in the USA.

City facts

The city undergoes a demographic explosion.

The peripheral railroad system begins operation.
1912

Population & demography

Detroit is organized into neighborhoods by ethnicity, representing various waves of migration.

The city urban fabric is characterized by low-density urban model and single-family isolated housing.

Social segregation is reinforced by public transportation and urban services.

21,019
45,619
79,577
116,340
205,876
285,704
542,452
465,766
725,064

1850
1900
1910

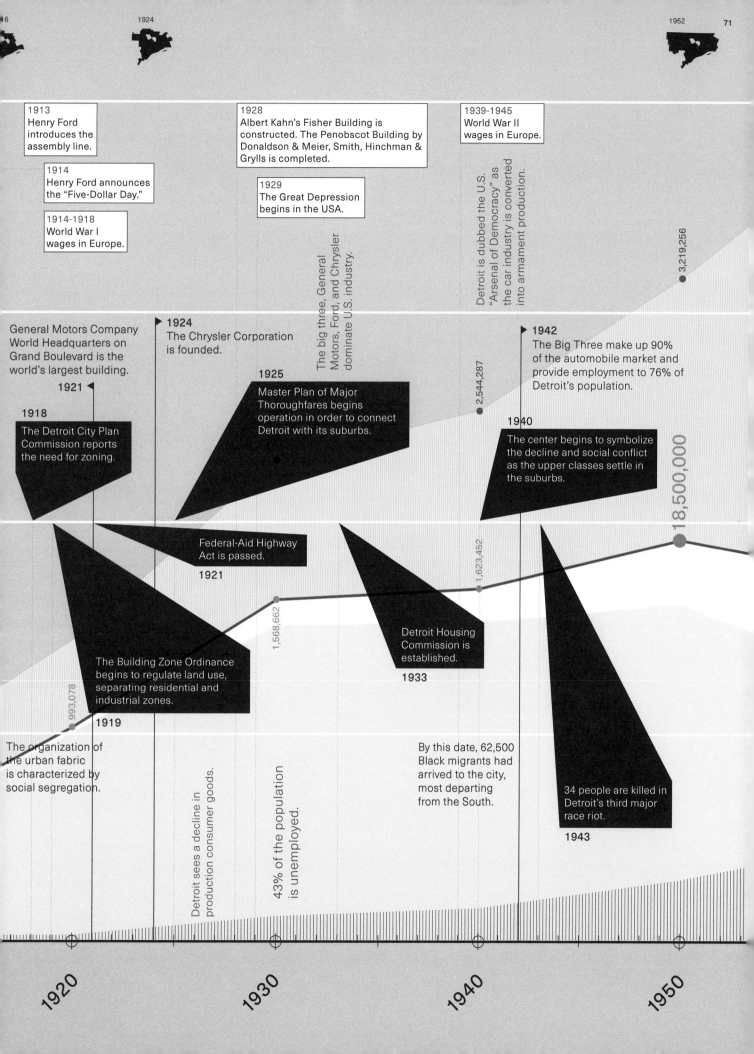

1913
Henry Ford introduces the assembly line.

1914
Henry Ford announces the "Five-Dollar Day."

1914-1918
World War I wages in Europe.

1928
Albert Kahn's Fisher Building is constructed. The Penobscot Building by Donaldson & Meier, Smith, Hinchman & Grylls is completed.

1929
The Great Depression begins in the USA.

1939-1945
World War II wages in Europe.

Detroit is dubbed the U.S. "Arsenal of Democracy" as the car industry is converted into armament production.

3,219,256

General Motors Company World Headquarters on Grand Boulevard is the world's largest building.
1921 ◀

1918
The Detroit City Plan Commission reports the need for zoning.

▶ 1924
The Chrysler Corporation is founded.

1925
Master Plan of Major Thoroughfares begins operation in order to connect Detroit with its suburbs.

The big three, General Motors, Ford, and Chrysler dominate U.S. industry.

2,544,287

▶ 1942
The Big Three make up 90% of the automobile market and provide employment to 76% of Detroit's population.

1940
The center begins to symbolize the decline and social conflict as the upper classes settle in the suburbs.

Federal-Aid Highway Act is passed.
1921

1,623,452

18,500,000

The Building Zone Ordinance begins to regulate land use, separating residential and industrial zones.
1919

1,568,662

Detroit Housing Commission is established.
1933

993,078

The organization of the urban fabric is characterized by social segregation.

Detroit sees a decline in production consumer goods.

43% of the population is unemployed.

By this date, 62,500 Black migrants had arrived to the city, most departing from the South.

34 people are killed in Detroit's third major race riot.
1943

1920   1930   1940   1950

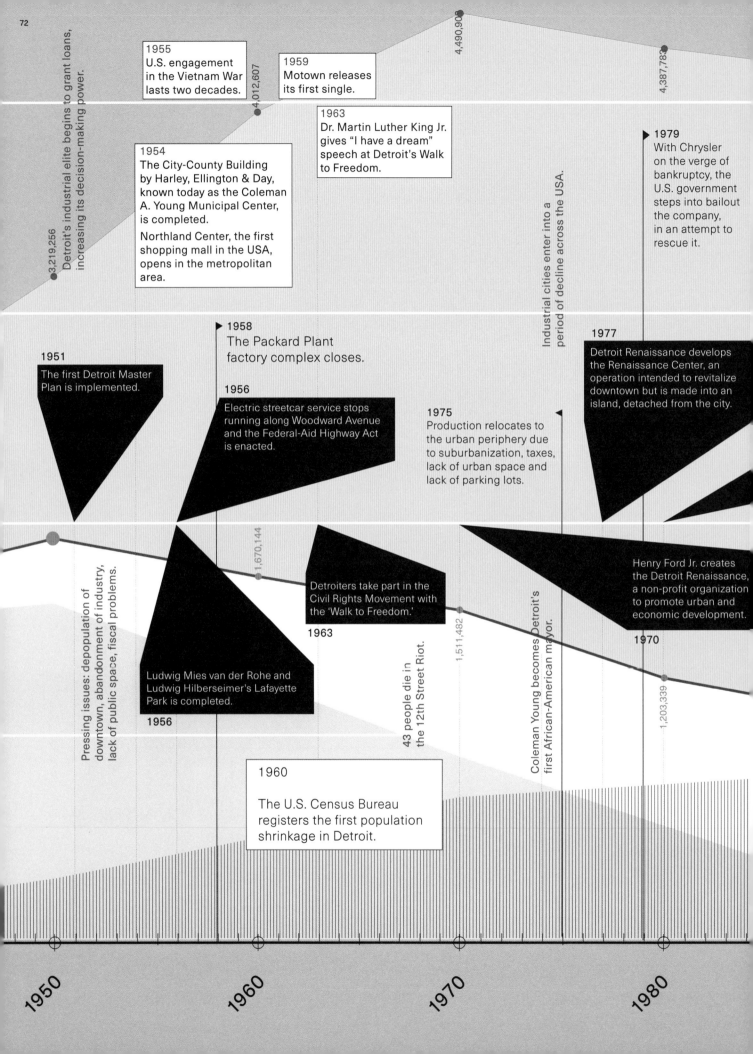

3,219,256

Detroit's industrial elite begins to grant loans, increasing its decision-making power.

4,012,607

1955
U.S. engagement in the Vietnam War lasts two decades.

1959
Motown releases its first single.

1963
Dr. Martin Luther King Jr. gives "I have a dream" speech at Detroit's Walk to Freedom.

1954
The City-County Building by Harley, Ellington & Day, known today as the Coleman A. Young Municipal Center, is completed.

Northland Center, the first shopping mall in the USA, opens in the metropolitan area.

4,490,90

4,387,78

1979
With Chrysler on the verge of bankruptcy, the U.S. government steps into bailout the company, in an attempt to rescue it.

Industrial cities enter into a period of decline across the USA.

1951
The first Detroit Master Plan is implemented.

1958
The Packard Plant factory complex closes.

1956
Electric streetcar service stops running along Woodward Avenue and the Federal-Aid Highway Act is enacted.

1975
Production relocates to the urban periphery due to suburbanization, taxes, lack of urban space and lack of parking lots.

1977
Detroit Renaissance develops the Renaissance Center, an operation intended to revitalize downtown but is made into an island, detached from the city.

1,670,144

Detroiters take part in the Civil Rights Movement with the 'Walk to Freedom.'

1963

Pressing issues: depopulation of downtown, abandonment of industry, lack of public space, fiscal problems.

Ludwig Mies van der Rohe and Ludwig Hilberseimer's Lafayette Park is completed.

1956

43 people die in the 12th Street Riot.

1,511,482

Coleman Young becomes Detroit's first African-American mayor.

Henry Ford Jr. creates the Detroit Renaissance, a non-profit organization to promote urban and economic development.

1970

1,203,339

1960

The U.S. Census Bureau registers the first population shrinkage in Detroit.

1950   1960   1970   1980

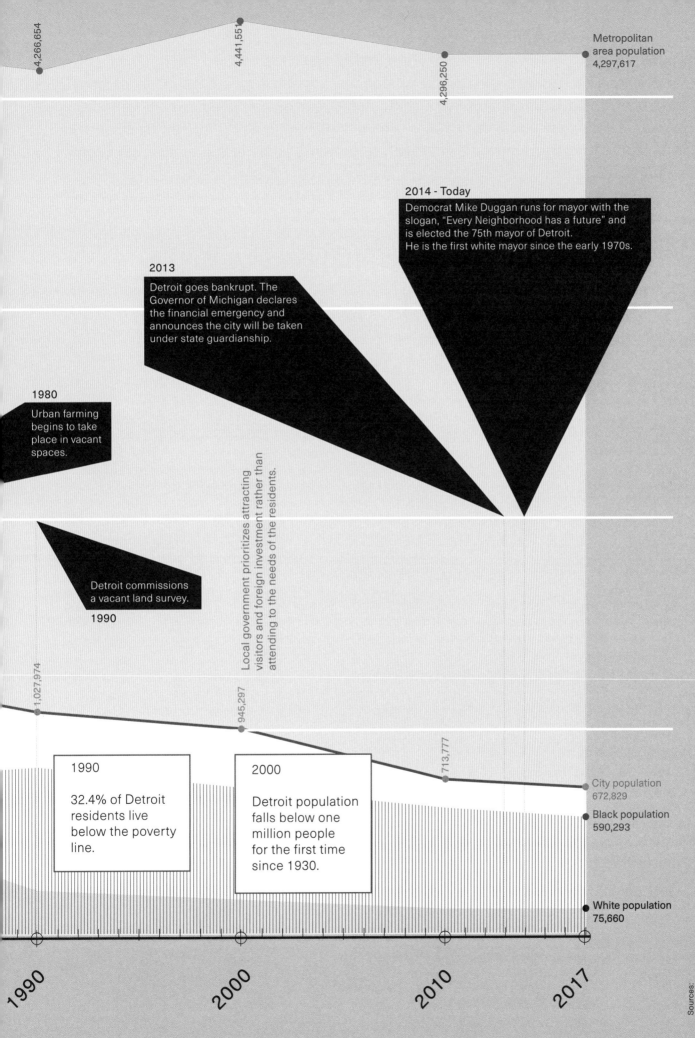

4,266,654

4,441,551

4,296,250

Metropolitan
area population
4,297,617

2014 - Today
Democrat Mike Duggan runs for mayor with the
slogan, "Every Neighborhood has a future" and
is elected the 75th mayor of Detroit.
He is the first white mayor since the early 1970s.

2013
Detroit goes bankrupt. The
Governor of Michigan declares
the financial emergency and
announces the city will be taken
under state guardianship.

1980
Urban farming
begins to take
place in vacant
spaces.

Local government prioritizes attracting
visitors and foreign investment rather than
attending to the needs of the residents.

Detroit commissions
a vacant land survey.
1990

1,027,974

945,297

713,777

1990

32.4% of Detroit
residents live
below the poverty
line.

2000

Detroit population
falls below one
million people
for the first time
since 1930.

City population
672,829

Black population
590,293

White population
75,660

1990 **2000** **2010** **2017**

Sources:
Detroit Public Schools. Dept. of Social Studies. "Detroit: A Manual for Citizens." Detroit: Board of Education of the City of Detroit, Michigan University, 1958. / Jaime Castilla Santos, extended by the research of Beatríz Fernández Águeda and Jerry Herron. Castilla Santos, Jaime. "Searching for Sugar Land." Koozarch, April 2017. Available online. / Fernández Águeda, Beatríz. "Futuros urbanos: la reversibilidad del proceso de deterioro". Madrid: Departamento de Urbanística y Ordenación del Territorio, ETSA Madrid, 2013. / Jerry Herron, "Chronology: Detroit since 1700". In: "Working paper: Complete Works 1 - Detroit". Available online. / Detroit Future City. Publications Special Reports in site of Detroit Future City. Available online. / United States Census Bureau. Available online.

To meet such a forward-thinking and clear-minded architect, whose career is defined by the ability to get involved both in academic speculations and 'muddy politics,' is rare, unique, and makes us wonder about the potential impact of these practices. Maurice Cox is the Director of the Planning and Development Department for the City of Detroit.[1] His transdisciplinary way of understanding the city, informed by what feels like a contemporary humanistic approach, is breaking some of the eroded conceptual grounds of urbanism.

PABLO GERSON

Planning + Delivering & Implementing

An Interview with Maurice Cox

PABLO GERSON

I would like to ask you briefly about your background, your training, and your position at the Planning and Development Department

MAURICE COX

I was educated as an architect at the Irwin S. Chanin School of Architecture at The Cooper Union in New York and I spent ten years living and practicing in Florence, Italy. I am not only coming from an intense urban environment like New York, but I also happen to have experience in urbanism in Europe, which is pretty singular. I think that formed who I am, relative to my belief in the significance of history, the importance of the public realm, the importance of architecture in its cultural contribution, and the role of an architect: more public citizens, very entrepreneurial, hosting workshops, public debates, publications ... It is a much more entrepreneurial framing of the architect as compared to the American architect, who has a more market-driven notion of practice. It was also the first time that I met a planning director of a major city: Massimo Carmassi, who is an architect. I was in my twenties and something that really surprised me back then is that an architect could be the director of an entire city.

I stored that memory away and when I got the call from Mike Duggan, it was not so strange to me that they were asking an architect to be the city's planning director.

When I came back to the USA from Italy and settled in Charlottesville, Virginia, I immediately got immersed in the cultural life of that city and found myself elected to public office. I served on the city council for six years. Soon after, I was elected mayor of the city. The entire time, I was teaching architecture and urbanism at the University of Virginia. I began to see the city in a much more complex way and understand the strategic role of the academy—using the city as a living laboratory. That is an important connection because often people who operate in the academy do not really like the rough-and-tumble of politics, but I was doing both simultaneously and I think that formed me. I subsequently became the Design Director for the National Endowment for the Arts, which gave me a national platform.

I also ran a program called the Mayors' Institute on City Design[2] that educated mayors on the power of their position to influence urban design—the urban form of the cities. I literally personally tutored over two hundred mayors over the three-year period.

After that, I went down to New Orleans to work as Social Dean for Community Engagement for Tulane University and ran a nonprofit design center that basically helped nonprofit organizations in their aspirations to rebuild the city better, post-Katrina.

That is when Mayor Mike Duggan, here

in Detroit, found me. He called really kind of out of the blue and recruited me for this job. That kind of trajectory is fairly important because I think the fact that I was a former mayor, that I had basically walked in his shoes, that I knew, not only the importance of planning, but also the importance of delivering and implementing—I guess I was the right person for the task. So, I left a ten-year position at Tulane to take a political appointment that could have been a two-year ride, and Mike Duggan is now up for reelection in November,[3] so hopefully we will get four more years to work this out.

URBAN FABRIC AND VACANT LAND

PG   You mentioned the importance of history. How do you understand Detroit and its role in the nation over the last century? How do you see that process developing, from the early 1900s?

MC   Detroit was subject to an astronomical population growth, filled by the re-imagining of the auto industry where hundreds of thousands of people, in very short order, moved to Detroit in search of the American Dream and employment. If we saw that kind of population growth today, we would say that it is totally unsustainable. And yet, it happened here in the first half of the

Ph. Fernando Schapochnik

twentieth century. In the second half, the transformation of the auto industry went through another cycle: this time, instead of building factories vertically in the city, they built them horizontally in the suburbs because they were in search of space. Really, already from the fifties, the population began to decline; it went from 1,800,000 to today, just under 700,000. But at the same time, the physical square mileage of the city did not shrink, just its population. Imagine a city where 1,100,000 people upped and left, and left their houses, their churches, their schools, the stores, empty! Imagine a city with a tax base that shrank so quickly over a fifty-year period that they were unable to provide basic services, neglecting all of those buildings.

Here we are today, with one of the largest inventories of historic structures left vacant in the nation. Here we are today, with more square miles of vacant land, publicly owned. It is about 24 square miles, which is larger than the island of Manhattan, and it is all under a single ownership, the Land Bank Authority.[4] That represents an unprecedented opportunity to rethink the American City, and in some very profound ways, because the pattern of vacancy is not contiguous in the way that Central Park public land is. For example, the island in Detroit called Belle Isle Park is larger than Central Park. How do you create or rethink a city without a specific pattern of land use? That is part of the challenge.

How do you create areas of density in a city that was built around the single-family house that symbolizes the American Dream? You have to remember that 80% of the housing stock in Detroit was built before 1960, which means that they were largely single-family units. Since the sixties, the city has been managing population decline. So, a lot of the urban housing and the urban innovations that have happened over the past sixty years

1.   The Planning and Development Department of the City of Detroit is split up into three strategical design regions, each lead by a Design Director. The Central Zone is piloted by Steven Lewis, the East Zone by Esther Yang and the West Zone by David Walker. The Design Directors provide planning, design leadership, and coordination, with the goal of achieving neighborhood stabilization, revitalization, and supporting the growth of population and jobs.

2.   The Mayors' Institute on City Design (MICD) is a leadership initiative of the National Endowment for the Arts in partnership with the United States Conference of Mayors. Since 1986, the Mayors' Institute has helped transform communities through design by preparing mayors to be the chief urban designers of their cities.

3.   Incumbent Mike Duggan won re-election to a second term on November 7th 2017, which will end in 2021.

4.   The Detroit Land Bank Authority is an agency that has acquired tens of thousands of city-owned properties, vacant lands, and abandoned properties, with the aim to redevelop. The city-led program is a rehabilitation or demolition through blight elimination program.

kind of passed over Detroit.

And that also represents an unusual opportunity: how do you build dense urban centers that are medium density, that can sit in the context of single-family houses? How do you connect those places to the other amenities that people have when they think of urban neighborhoods: parks, schools, libraries, shopping districts? How do you connect all of that, through a network of greenways, that are not like Central Park? These are those greenways where people still live. They are maybe half a dozen houses on a block but they are surrounded by vacant land. How do you create an urban experience? How do you create, within a rural context, or how do you create a rural context within an urban city? Those are some of the challenges. I would argue that there are only two or three precedents: first ring suburbs, at the beginning of twentieth century, kind of City Beautiful where there are these beautiful little villages and very leafy green environments served usually by street cars; there is the American suburb which

sprawls in big lots and which is almost all auto-oriented. Then, you have rural lands, where the land is productive, the density is very low, but one would argue that there is an economic model that makes some sense and is quite beautiful.

That is what we are exploring: how to create a variety of ways of living in the city. If you want to live in a rural environment you can live in a rural environment, get on an express bus and get downtown in 15 minutes. Or, if you live in an urban environment, you can walk within 20 minutes to all those services that you might normally expect in an urban environment.

I think it is interesting, while there are several precedents and existing typologies, we get to pilot this idea on 139 square miles.

BOTTOM UP STRATEGIES

PG   Detroit has been going through all of those development processes you

described since the fifties. Regarding that matter, what do you think about participative urbanism?

MC   Part of the reason why I took the job is because Detroit has a history of incredible resilience and a bottom-up problem solving. Basically, nobody was coming to the rescue here. The government was not coming to the rescue, local government did not work as it should, and people just basically took the recovery into their own hands and built a set of skills to take over and work the land. If your neighbors have left, you start growing things in the vacant land, or, if your block is empty, you start mowing the grass on the land near your house. People have really found ways to keep a level of regeneration going, and very often it is not coordinated, it does not have the benefit of synergy, and certainly does not have the benefit of what the government can do, which is much more systems based, which can amplify the work. The Heidelberg Project[5] which is a well-known art installation, has been going on for 30 years by artists in Detroit neighborhoods, originally transforming houses through art as a way to bring attention to blight. And it became a really important tourist destination. Now, the city, through my office, is entering into a memorandum of understanding with that organization to try to help them to become a community developer of that area. Lift up a local culture and provide them with the partnership that government can provide. I could tell you dozens of organizations that the city could partner with as a way to return those neighborhoods to their authentic identity, but also with the idea of bringing a level of technical resource that could transform neighborhoods. Again, there are many examples of this nationally; what Detroit has is an opportunity to do it on a large scale and to do it many times over. I think that is when you start to get a collective identity through these specific interventions, with art and culture as a main center.

POSTINDUSTRIALISM

PG   There is a radical change in our time regarding the approaches to the problematic of postindustrial cities that need new planning strategies. In that sense, Detroit could work as a model within the United States. What is the role of planning in this specific context?

MC   I think that planning today has no other choice but to use the resources of those who are already there to collectively solve problems. I don't think that planners, professionally, whether they be landscape architects, architects, city planners, or urbanists, can do this without the people who are there. Mainly because, who are you planning for? And if you are a planner, if you are not planning for some mythical demographic sect that is going to come and save your city, then you are planning for the people who are there, who have stuck it out with your city. In the particular case of Detroit, it is even more pronounced. Detroit has an unusual situation where around 700,000 people

"Design is the ultimate political act of intention and to design in the public interest is where you can have the greatest impact."

who are here, are really the hard-core group that would not go.
You have a group of people, when I call a community meeting, who have been in their homes for forty, fifty, sixty years. Clearly, they are the ones who know the identity of their neighborhoods, they are the ones who can remember a time where their neighborhoods were healthy, and they are the ones who are not going anywhere. It helps our work tremendously to have people who have lived a very long time in a place; they are also the first ones to welcome new people. It is part of the regeneration. On the other hand, you need an infusion in the new neighborhoods that are not growing, generally perceived to be, "If you are not growing, are you dying? Are you stagnant?" I think there are different notions of growth because, how do you grow a neighborhood when you are not going to build another single-family house?
We have a couple of these urban neighborhood laboratories and we are trying to come up with strategies to regenerate those neighborhoods without building a single new structure.
In one case, we have 160 acres, or a quarter square mile, where there are about 600 families that still live there. There are about 135 vacant houses and there are about 200 vacant lots in these 25 acres of vacant land. What if we could rid that quarter square mile and demolish the houses that cannot be recuperated, we will renovate every single one of the houses that are vacant, which number about 115, and then we can plant gardens on every vacant lot in the neighborhood. We will take some of those vacant lands

and see if we can make a very intentional multi-eco park. We will take other pieces of those vacant parcels and string them together, with the idea that they can form a greenway, with walking and biking gardens through the neighborhoods; we will develop a typology of different ways for vacant lots to be activated in order to be productive and we will ask a single community developer to work on the whole thing and employ people who are in the neighborhoods to install and maintain these gardens. That project is on the way, it was approved and even the framework has won several awards for the landscape architects that brought it together for us. We are going to break ground on this park by the end of 2017. This is the kind of question I am talking about on regeneration, that is a very unconventional way of thinking about how to grow a neighborhood, but is what we have to do. In order to get to a point to operate at that scale, we have to bring along an entire neighborhood. What was dozens and dozens of meetings with residents trying to figure this out, trying to get them to understand that planting a garden is another form of regeneration. That if we can't provide a new house for a family with children, we can rehab a house and put a family with children there, or we can build a house on a vacant parcel. We can also bring in a neighborhood-friendly land-based business that will help create a neighborhood. When we realized that we could make this 'make sense financially' and that the developer could actually make a profit, we put it out for a request proposal and we got a very unconventional developer who said

5.   The Heidelberg Project is an outdoor art environment in the heart of an urban area; it is a Detroit-based community organization with a mission to improve neighborhoods and the lives of the people that live there, through art.

"yeah, I can do this." And now, if you can do it in this neighborhood, could you do it in another one?

We have now found at least three other neighborhoods with a similar house/ vacant land ratio. We are going to be putting that out for 2017 and early 2018. And what is important here is that I could not go to another city and say: we have a city, renovated with over 100 homes and planted 20 hectares of gardens, it just doesn't exist. We had to make this up.

Getting back to the issue of design excellence and impact: the design of this strategy was done by an Australian landscape architect, Elizabeth Mossop, partnering with a local architecture firm, Loeb Fellow Dan Pitera.[6]

Before we went out to look for the developer and his potential idea, we actually commissioned the framework, designed it in this entirety, priced it out, and then we sent it out to the developer and asked, "Can you implement this?"

It ended up being a very proactive way of not just looking to developers to give us the answer, but conceiving the answer collectively with residents, with some of the best design professionals possible, and then asking the developers to implement the strategy. I am trying to illustrate to you how important the engagement was, and the proactive vision of the city and the planning department was, before the developer was called to come in and share their expertise.

UNRULED RULES FOR EQUITY

PG   Going back to what you said before, why do you think architects haven't built a disciplinary field that is engaged in decision-making, like you are doing here?

MC   European architects have historically been engaged in politics or been part of a public discourse about the built environment, but I think that the architectural education in America has been, at times, sort of apolitical. There was a time in the sixties when architects were out there trying to solve problems and responding to the urban crises. At a certain point, they parted ways, and you saw the emergence of the academic architect, the star architect who can only operate if they have millions and millions of dollars and they are designing a museum; there was a movement away from architects being problem solvers, of architects being combiners.

When I came back to the USA, within three years I ran for public office, largely because I thought I had an expertise that was of value or could be of value to the city. I did not have a platform; my opinion was no more valuable than a shop owner down the street. I just thought that I could do something about that—I am going to get into a position where I am not just responding to the rules, I am writing the rules.

There has always been a kind of an activist streak in designers, but they love to design, they are not all of these other tangential issues that impact design. They would rather not bother with those. And you can understand, they come from a creative place and they just want to make beautiful stuff. I think that is a fairly naive approach, because design is the ultimate political act of intention and to design in the public interest is where you can have the greatest impact. I have pretty much come to believe that access to healthy—socially, economically—vibrant environments should be a birthright for someone born in a democratic country. It is no different, in my mind, than access to good public education, or, the expectation of access to good public health. It is a right. Living in a socially, economically, environmentally, healthy neighborhood, it's a right!

If that is the case, it colors everything that I do relative to design as a question of equity. Why should only wealthy neighborhoods have access to quality streetscapes, quality shopping districts, or housing options? Shouldn't all parts of our city aspire to that? I believe that Detroit is the kind of place where we can pull that off.

6.   Dan Pitera is an architect and political and social activist. He is now the Executive Director of the Detroit Collaborative Design Center at the University of Detroit Mercy School of Architecture. He was a Loeb Fellow (2005) at Harvard University, as Maurice Cox (2005) and Steven Lewis (2007).

Architecture and social engagement run in his blood. Brought up in upstate New York, Steven Lewis started working with his father in Harlem. He is now one of the Urban Design Director of the Center Region of Detroit. He uses his sensibility and humor to empathize and strengthen the community network. In this interview, he tells us more about the design strategies behind the latest challenges facing Detroit: countering land vacancy, serving and building the city's population, and boosting the economy.

PABLO GERSON

Towards a 'Mix Tape' Detroit

An Interview with Steven Lewis

PABLO GERSON

Since you came to Detroit, you've been working hard to support neighborly initiatives and empower the community. I would like to know more about your background before you arrived to this office.

STEVEN LEWIS

I got my degree in 1979 from Syracuse University and worked immediately for my father, who was also an architect. He grew up in Harlem and when he was able to establish his own practice in 1970 with two partners, they focused on neighborhoods within Harlem and other urban areas in decay, mainly because the U.S. Department of Housing and Urban Development launched its Section 8 Housing Program[1] and the Section 202 Senior Housing Programs concentrated on redeveloping inner cities. After several months, I went to Los Angeles to work with my uncle, who also happened to be an architect, but soon after I was able to get a job—quite over my head as far as experience—at the re-development agency in Los Angeles. Because of my background at my father's practice, I essentially made a leap over a lot of my peers in my age group. In the mid-nineties, a close friend and associate—Joe Osae Addo—and I produced a revolutionary design for the federal government that was entered into the GSA Design Excellence Award program.[2] Successfully winning one of the awards led me to get to know the head of that office, Chief Archi-

tect Ed Feiner. In the sixties and seventies, federal architecture was so bad that none of the good architects would even pursue it. But when he came in, he re-arranged it and it began to attract the best and brightest architects. So, now you can see a legacy of two decades of wonderful federal civic architecture, from border stations to federal office buildings, and headquarter houses. As Maurice Cox looked at the candidates for my current position, he immediately thought about me because of my large project experience with the federal government. I am one of the three urban design directors that have jurisdiction over the entire 139 squares miles of the city. In order to manage that much geography, we felt it was necessary to divide it into three areas: East, West, and Central. There is David Walker in the West, Esther Yang in the East, and myself. Our approaches are all very relationship-driven. When we go out in the neighborhoods, we go out with a great deal of empathy, a great deal of compassion, and none of the baggage that we would carry if we were native Detroiters. If we came from here, we would be burned with all of its history. We have a clean slate to work with as we go out to build trust with the people in the neighborhoods.

PG   What was the department's situation when you arrived here in Detroit?

SL   Back in the fifties, Charles Blessing was the director of the Planning Department

and, as I read in "Redevelopment and Race" by June Manning Thomas, an account of his ten years in office, he was aspirational and visionary in the same way that Maurice Cox is.[3] However, the good works were never able to get teeth to really take hold, I think largely because of federal policy and, ultimately, racism. Therefore, we see what we see: the departure from the city, the decline, and the ironic effects of the 1965 Housing Act under Lyndon B. Johnson.[4] The ability of those who had been sequestered within a boundary of what was allowed to be a Black community also got out, and what they left behind in their wake was a concentration of poverty, hopelessness, and despair, which continues until today. It was ironic that before then, you could be the wealthiest Black brain surgeon, like Dr. Ben Carson, or a drug dealer, and you would live in the same neighborhood; all of the dollars were recirculated within the neighborhood because the businesses were Black-owned.[5] Then Urban Renewal came along—otherwise known as 'negro removal'—where the freeway came in and wiped out what was, in Detroit, the most vital artery of commerce: Hastings Street. It was replaced with an express route, the Chrysler Freeway, constructed in order to get people in and out of the suburbs as efficiently as possible. The planning department in which Maurice walked into was an almost Kafkaesque situation of people just stamping things like demolition permits; there was no vision

Ph. Fernando Schapochnik

at all. There was no collective sense of possibility or resources mainly because bankruptcy was so terrible for this city. But emerging out of it, as a kind of phoenix rising from the ashes, you have Mayor Mike Duggan with a new and different vision. Not to shrink the city but to grow the city by increasing its population. Not by proliferating it throughout 139 square miles, which is not sustainable, but rather to concentrate new population in viable centers of neighborhoods with commercial quarters that can support new mixed-use ground level retails with housing above. He tried to start to turn the curve on parking so that it does not dominate the landscape.

Along with my professional activity at the planning department, I am co-teaching a design studio which allows us to bring a real project from here into the design studio. My class, "Designing with Community," is a primer on getting alerted to the skills it takes to actually make meaningful community engagement a cornerstone of the planning work that we do.

Honestly, the other part of my background

is because of my DNA. My father's codes were, by nature, socially-conscious. No one in the profession was paying attention to the conditions or situations in low-income Black neighborhoods. When someone needed something, they would always find my dad or one of his colleagues through the network. We were doing 'public interest design'—as it is called today. It is funny and ironic that it is becoming a kind of mainstream. The younger white professionals who are involved in public interest design think it has just arrived or that it has just been discovered. There is no memory, there

is no history, no legacy, it goes back to the issue within the profession that we are so invisible as people of color. In 1971, Whitney M. Young Jr., who was a key civil rights leader, was asked to address the American Institute of Architects. He really slammed the institute for having all of this talent and skills that preferred to pursue commissions for beautiful buildings instead of using any of it to remedy the ills of the inner cities. At that point, Black architects represented a mere two percent of the profession, of licensed architects. Today, in 2017, Black architects represent two percent of the pro-

1   Section 8 is a common name for the Housing Choice Voucher Program. It allowed tenants to use rental housing assistance to pay private landlords for low-income households.

2   U.S. General Services Administration, GSA is an independent government agency that was established to help manage and support the basic functioning of federal agencies.

3   Charles Blessing served as Director of City Planning in Detroit from 1953 to 1977. He initiated the large-scale housing project known as Lafayette Park.

4   The Housing and Urban Development Act of 1965 was a major revision to federal housing policy in the United States; it instituted several major expansions in federal housing programs. This act extended the urban renewal programs set in motion by the 1949 act, which provided various forms of federal assistance to cities for removing dilapidated housing and redeveloping parts of downtowns.

5   Ben Carson is an American neurosurgeon, author, and politician who is currently the U.S. Secretary of Housing and Urban Development.

fession. Nothing there has changed.

PG   As you said earlier, Cox, yourself, and the team were foreign to Detroit. What were the first strategies you thought of when you encountered this huge and complex city?

SL   I think the basic strategy is locating the areas that have the most strength and viability. If you can densify and increase population there by increasing surfaces, those nodes can then start to grow together. But key to the entire strategy for Detroit is within exactly that question: what do you do with all the vacant land?
We have a tremendous amount of vacant land that has to be rethought. In our case, we are piloting a number of experiments for the conversion of that land to some land-based business. These strategies for land stewardship are immensely important and therefore we have been able to attract some of the brightest talents globally in landscape architecture. In particular, Elizabeth Mossop was awarded and got a contract for the Fitzgerald neighborhoods.[6] There was a competition, a process that Maurice Cox has made really transparent. The selection no longer happens behind closed doors, they are mostly done in some public form and the press is kind in covering it.
I think that a huge challenge for us is the narrative, the prevailing narratives that are out there. Longtime-residents of African-American neighborhoods like to say "oh, what is happening downtown? That is for them, not for us..." But we can counter that narrative by just walking down the street and seeing the foosball table with a couple of brothers. Wherever you look, there are Black people occupying and using public space as well as White people. It is a constant all hands-on deck to counter those narratives, not to ignore them but to listen really carefully to what people are saying, to gather the legitimacy of their thoughts and complaints, and then try to understand how to address it.
When we go to community meetings and we start speaking to the neighbors, I am speaking to my cousin, my uncle, my grandmother, and they are looking at their son or their nephew. There is, through this cultural

congruity, a channel of communication. We have to convince them that we are in fact genuine and very self-determined in looking out for their interest but not without their fundamental input. There is an adage—no idea who it is attributed to—it says, "nothing about us is without us, it is for us," which is a beautiful concept for true engagement.

PG   Governments are usually unreachable, but just recently I read something really interesting regarding the accessibility to government information in the city of Detroit; how does it work?

SL   Our office has been really accessible to the public, others perhaps not as much. I think it is less a matter of being able to access it as it is the systems that are still in a place that seem like they were created just to be a roadblock to getting anything done. We are re-writing zoning, re-visiting codes to try to make things a lot easier. This 'mix tape' project that Maurice has got an asset to, started as an entitle of Pink Zoning Detroit,[7] which is about delaying the red tape and making it pink so that you can start to bring down some of the bureaucracy. 'Mix tape' is the new name for it—that came from the community members.

PG   Public-private partnerships seem to be the key economic strategies for urban development, how is it in Detroit? And, which are the projects the department is currently involved in?

SL   My own experience with public-private partnerships so far has been mostly through philanthropy, working with a group like the Detroit RiverFront Conservancy, to amass funds that allow for the hiring of the top-edge design firms to do visioning for the riverfront. In this case, it was awarded to SOM that is working on a long term project.[8] However, we can only really speak about what we can deliver based on known funding sources within an amount of four or five years, maximum. This is also about rebuilding trust. In the public-private partnership, the public has to be able to offer something. Right now, we have land that is probably our biggest asset, and up until recently most of that land was devalued.

Hopefully this year, there will be a good outcome for the city, where we get funds and we can go out in the process of fixing roads, creating, protecting, reducing, and putting those big fat roads on the 'road diet' as we call them. A 'road diet' will reduce the through-lanes, slow down the traffic, and make it safer to cross, giving people better access to the riverfront. So, there are tons of strategies being teed up but there haven't been any opportunities yet for a lot of them. In our department, we have basically been instructed that our priorities are in the neighborhoods. Those often aren't big fancy projects, they are mainly restoring basic infrastructure, fixing broken sidewalks, getting lighting in alleys, things that will make an immediate improvement on the daily quality of life of residents. Right now, the city is obligated to cut the vacant lawns four times a year to have a six-inch uniform mow on a lawn. What if you could take the money required for that and invest it in a strategy that would beautify the lot with some other kind of wild landscape. Then, you would just have to 'manicure' the edges and put a little kind of edge, like fences, in order to create some beauty and sustainability without having to just mow lawns.
There is one project in my district that is coming up called "Eastern Market," which they are now calling "Neighborhood Innovation Zone." It is intended to take all of the food production uses, the hardcore like slaughtering and other things, that by law have to be taken by the front door retail. Now, the market is really the heartbeat of the city. The market and the riverfront are the two major organs that pump life into the city with a vast diversity of people who come and flood it every Saturday and Tuesday. There is also a tremendous amount of vacant land, and we are going to create this new zone over there, and then figure out how to backfill that market space with food-related businesses that really intensify the vibrancy of that district, so maybe instead of just two days a week, it should be opened all week. At the same time, there is a demand for housing in that precise neighborhood as well. We are just about to award a $775,000 contract to a consulting team to do that work.
In the Arena District, for example, we just

opened up the new Caesar Arena. All four major sport teams are playing within the close geographic boundary of downtown and the 50-block area that they have planned. That happened before we came; we have at least an opportunity now to meet with them on a regular basis, to influence things, to try to balance the standard formula these large companies use as they march from city to city and put their stamp on it like "LA live" in Los Angeles. They wanted to do the same thing here, and we want something that is more uniquely authentic to Detroit.

Also, there is obviously Dan Gilbert and the Quicken Loans dynasty which I think is the single economic engine that initiated all the redevelopment here because he introduced employment into the downtown area.[9]

PG   Where is Detroit heading in the next fifteen years?

SL   I think that in ten or fifteen years from now, there will be a significant economic heartbeat in the city coming from larger corporate entities that decide to locate here due basically to the cost. As the cost is rising, we will hit a ceiling where we have to be competing with other places but, while it is still offering the amenities of an urban lifestyle, meaning that new businesses, enterprises, and retail are coming, we will continue to be attractive. People think "Detroit, no, no way," but if they look at it closely, it could offer some incredible potential for some big companies like Amazon, who can bring thousands and thousands of workers. That would be transformative. There is also a very supportive art community that works together and generates other types of collective spaces. I think that there has always been a grassroots maker's culture here. The downtown is the heart of the city, but the neighborhoods are its soul.

PLANNING AREAS

Detroit's Design Regions
Planning and Development Department

☐ Other Project Area
☐ Planning Project Underway
   Central Zone (Council Districts 6 and 7)
▨ East Zone (Council Districts 3, 4, and 5)
   West Zone (Council Districts 1 and 2)

Neighborhood-Based Development Project
Housing and Revitalization Department

▨ Multifamily Housing Study Area
● Business Develoment Projects
○ Motor City Match Design/Building/CashWinners
● Multifamily Housing Sites
▨ Real Estate Projects

Sources:
"Planning Areas", Planning Division, General & Strategic Planning, Planning and Development Department of the City of Detroit.
City of Detroit, "Neighborhood-Based Development Projects", Building Detroit, Detroit Land Bank Authority. Available online.

6   See more about the Fitzgerald Revitalization Project on p. 84.
7   Pink Zoning Detroit seeks to transform Detroit's complex land use regulations into a positive force for neighborhood revitalization.
8   See more about the Detroit East Riverfront Framework Plan on p. 86.
9   Dan Gilbert is the chairman and founder of Quicken Loans, a mortgage lending company located in the financial district of downtown Detroit.

The Detroit office of the Australian firm Spackman Mossop Michaels looks to transform a quarter square mile area by addressing every publicly-owned vacant lot and house in the Fitzgerald Revitalization Project Area. The strategy will focus on removing blighted structures, beautifying vacant lots, and creating homes for new residents in order to contribute to overall stability, increase property values, and improve quality of life.

SPACKMAN MOSSOP MICHAELS

Fitzgerald Revitalization Project

Landscape as the Framework for Community Reinvestment

Neighborhoods in Detroit are dealing with the impact of blighted and vacant properties in their communities. Spackman Mossop Michaels was commissioned by the City of Detroit to envision a bold new way to address distressed neighborhoods by focusing on the landscape of the entire area rather than addressing blighted properties on a lot-by-lot basis.

The Fitzgerald Project Area, located within the Fitzgerald neighborhood in North Detroit, was selected for this pilot projects because of the concentration of publicly-owned vacant lots and homes. Currently, the vacancy rate in the neighborhood is around 50%, with over three hundred vacant parcels in the square mile area. The plan is made up of four primary initiatives: the Ella Fitzgerald Park, a new community park with access to the Fitzgerald Greenway, which connects the two universities on either end of the neighborhood; the Landscape Stewardship Plan, a public-private partnership to develop affordable housing; and the Productive Landscapes Initiative, a public-private partnership to

encourage market-driven landscape-based businesses. Those initiatives also serve as opportunities to provide employment. The Green Conservation Corps, in partnership with the Greening of Detroit, hires local residents to work on low-maintenance landscapes, ensuring that the spaces are well kept over the long term. The project also renovates dozens of houses currently owned by the City of Detroit, converting them into renovated homes for families and demolishing those that cannot be saved.

Early on, the City of Detroit committed to a transparent process in which neighborhood residents are involved in every step of the project. The community takes part in the selection of the Community Development Team, which implements most of the plan and simultaneously addresses multiple interconnected issues, including landscape strategies, workforce development, crime reduction, and affordable housing. The Request for Proposal for a Community Development Team aims to rehabilitate 115 of the existing structures to create affordable

housing; the Landscape Stewardship Plan uses the same development team to implement and maintain landscape interventions on the two hundred or more vacant lots in the neighborhood.

Of the 373 parcels of land, fifty will be used towards creating new public community spaces in the new Ella Fitzgerald Park and the Fitzgerald Greenway, and over two hundred will be part of the Landscape Stewardship Plan. Analysis and inventory of the existing land assets in the Fitzgerald neighborhood determined the best uses of these vacant lots. Factors such as size, distribution, adjacency, ownership status, and community character were compiled and evaluated. Out of this process, Spackman Mossop Michaels developed lot treatment typologies and strategies for unbuilt and underutilized land that deploy sustainable maintenance strategies and contribute to neighborhood stabilization and revitalization, with the aim of encouraging a positive identity and improving environmental performance.

DATE: 2016 – 2017 / LOCATION: Fitzgerald neighborhood, Detroit, Michigan / SITE AREA: 160 acres / CLIENT: City of Detroit / STATUS: Completed / DESIGN TEAM: Wes Michaels, Elizabeth Mossop, Emily Bullock, Liz Camuti, Jane Satterlee, Katie Boutte, Matty Williams / COLLABORATORS: Dan Pitera, Ceara O'Leary, Sarah Hayosh (Detroit Collaborative Design Center), Larry Weaner, Ethan Dropkin, Rebecca Kagle (Larry Weaner Landscape Associates), Lauren Hood (Live6 Alliance), Maurice Cox , Alexa Bush, Dave Walker , Cecily King, Kim Tandy, David Williams, Arthur Jemison (City of Detroit), University of Detroit Mercy, Marygrove College, Detroit Land Bank Authority, The Greening of Detroit, Fitzgerald Community Council College, Core Block Club, San Juan Block Club, Bethune Fitzgerald Academy / IMAGES: Courtesy of Spackman Mossop Michaels / spackmanmossopmichaels.com

LANDSCAPE STRATEGY : ENGAGEMENT SUMMARY

Greenways
— Secondary path
— Connect to college
— Connect to university
☐ Central Park

○ Gateway signage
▪ Gateway lighting
◯ Neighborhood Hub

▨ Grove (Along Green way)
▨ Crop (5-6 Lots)
▨ Orchard Typology (3-4 Lots)
▨ Meadow Typology (1-2 Lots)

ORCHARD TYPOLOGY

GROVE TYPOLOGY

CROP TYPOLOGY

MEADOW TYPOLOGY

CENTRAL PARK

GARDEN TYPOLOGY

GROVE
Traffic calming will reduce the speed of passing cars; greenway crosswalks will be designed as traffic tables to slow down cars and make the streets safer.

CROP
The city is seeking implementation partners for community land-based businesses that might make use of productive growing landscapes and other assets.

CENTRAL PARK
Central Park will include a multi-purpose sports field, playgrounds, exercise areas, and spaces for outdoor events.

GATEWAY SIGNAGE AND LIGHTING
Additional lighting is important for safety and to encourage the use of public space; gateway lighting is planned along the Greenway, at Neighborhood Hubs, key entry points, and in Central Park.

MEADOW TYPOLOGY
The project includes sidewalk repairs, as needed. The single lots identified as meadows will be installed and maintained by the housing developer.

Building on a ten-year initiative led by the Detroit RiverFront Conservancy, in collaboration with the City of Detroit Planning & Development Department and the Detroit Economic Growth Corporation (DEGC), architects and urban planners Skidmore, Owings & Merrill LLP (SOM), developed a framework plan for Detroit's East Riverfront District. The plan is designed to preserve riverfront land for public use, generate greater community access to the Detroit River, and spur investment along the East Riverfront.

SKIDMORE, OWINGS & MERRILL LLP (SOM)

Detroit East Riverfront Framework Plan

Redevelopment of the East Riverfront Area

In 2017, DEGC made a Request for Proposals to envision an adaptive reuse of the historic structure, increasing density on the waterfront. The outcome strategic framework plan by SOM forges new connections between the East Riverfront and surrounding neighborhoods, expands green space, and makes pedestrian-friendly streetscape improvements. Realized after an intensive six-month program of community meetings —workshops, tours, and interviews—it is the result of a public-private collaboration between the City of Detroit and the Detroit RiverFront Conservancy. The principal mission of the non-profit organization, founded in 2003, is to develop public access to Detroit's waterfront and serve as an anchor for economic development. It is responsible for raising the funds needed for construction, operation, on-time maintenance, security, and programming of public space.

The plan outlines the addition of eight acres of park space to the East Riverfront, envisions keeping significant portions of the waterfront free from private development in perpetuity, and confers a particular significance for short-time improvements in order to give the citizens safe access to the enhanced riverfront. Improvements along Jefferson Avenue would reduce vehicular accidents, improve walkability, and beautify the corridor; they are designed to support local businesses and facilitate waterfront access. The Beltline is a new greenway that will directly connect inland neighborhoods to the Detroit River; the existing Joseph Campau Greenway will receive new lighting, paving, and landscaping. The project is focused on four main aims: parks and green open spaces that are inclusive and accessible, safe and attractive greenways with sustainable streets for all residents, and facilitating local businesses and property development while preserving the heritage of the East Riverfront.

This requalification of the urban landscape also offers the possibility of regenerating natural habitat and offering new opportunities in terms of infrastructure, promenades, and management of natural components. Building a new East Riverfront with the citizen in mind is also a way to treat this wet area, supervising the water network and boosting citizens' awareness of environmental issues. The project seeks to continue transforming the East Riverfront area from a blighted, industrial area, into a vibrant, public waterfront, accessible to all Detroit residents.

DATE: 2017 / LOCATION: Detroit East Riverfront, Detroit, Michigan / SITE AREA: 480 acres / CLIENT: City of Detroit and the Detroit RiverFront Conservancy / STATUS: In process / DESIGN TEAM: Skidmore, Owings and Merrill (SOM) / COLLABORATORS: HR&A Advisors (urban economic development specialists), Michel Desvigne and Inessa Hansch (landscape architects), McIntosh Poris, Giffels Webster, Kraemer Design Group, AKT Peerless, Rich & Associates, E. Austell Associates / IMAGES: Courtesy of Skidmore, Owings & Merrill / som.com

Greenway connections and an expanded park space bridge nearby communities to the river, catalyzing investments that respect Detroit's history while embracing the identity of the district.

Detroit Riverwalk, view to the Renaissance Center.

"Searching for Sugar Land" is the result of an extensive and complex Final Thesis, completed at the Escuela Técnica Superior de Arquitectura de Madrid; it explores alternative understandings of the current state of Detroit and offers planning and design strategies for the future. The project proposes a global intervention in line with the territory's urgent state, reconnecting and boosting the urban fabric through interactions with its citizens and using new technological tools.

JAIME CASTILLA SANTOS

Searching for Sugar Land
Drawing the Hypercity Network

Jaime Castilla Santos places particular emphasis on the concept of a 'hypercity,' first proposed by the Swiss historian André Corboz[1] and related to the concept of 'metapolis,' which was coined by François Ascher.[2] A hypercity aspires to describe both a morphology and an urban sociology. Regarding the shape of the hypercity, Ascher postulates that it is heterogeneous and not necessarily constituted by contiguity—it loses the topological pattern of the traditional city and is characterized by the phenomenon of space fragmentation. A dynamic urban cartography establishes the pattern of architectural and urban development to pursue. Following a matrix of 500 by 500 meters within three categories (habitability and culture, production and innovation, and vegetation and energy), it identifies potentially prosperous landscapes. The outcome axonometric of the hypercity reveals a global and multi-scale vision of Detroit: selected fragments of the city work together simultaneously in the extended network of such a large mechanism. This transversal analysis allows global interventions for Detroit within an operative and open urban strategy. It also generates a catalog of strategies for trans-formation and improvements for isolated hubs of activities.

Detroit could become an archetype of urban regeneration. Through a strategic reactivation of the city, new landscapes would generate settlement models that are consistent with the environment and local resources. A sustainable and partici-patory urban model that would work for all Detroiters would be enabled by communi-cation modes and new technology.

For several decades, the citizens have been reinventing sustainable way of living through entrepreneurship, creativity, and collaborative work.

Detroit is considered a hub for industrial design and an art laboratory, making it no surprise that the city joined the UNESCO Creative City Network in 2015.

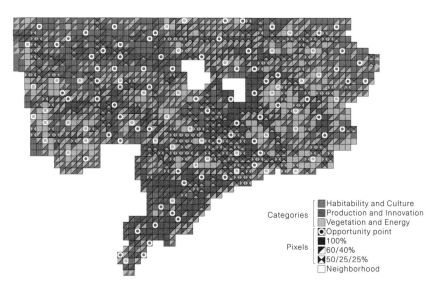

Categories: Habitability and Culture / Production and Innovation / Vegetation and Energy / Opportunity point

Pixels: 100% / 60/40% / 50/25/25% / Neighborhood

1.   Andre Corboz is a Swiss historian of art, architecture, and urban planning. Following his statement: the postindustrial city might be defined by its relation system more than by its own geometry system.
2.   François Ascher is a French urban planner and sociologist.

DATE: 2016-2017 / STATUS: Final Thesis , Escuela Técnica Superior de Arquitectura de Madrid. COLLABORATOR: Jorge Aritz Urgoiti Serrano. / IMAGES: Courtesy of Jaime Castilla Santos.

REPORT-NESS: DETROIT

BROWSER

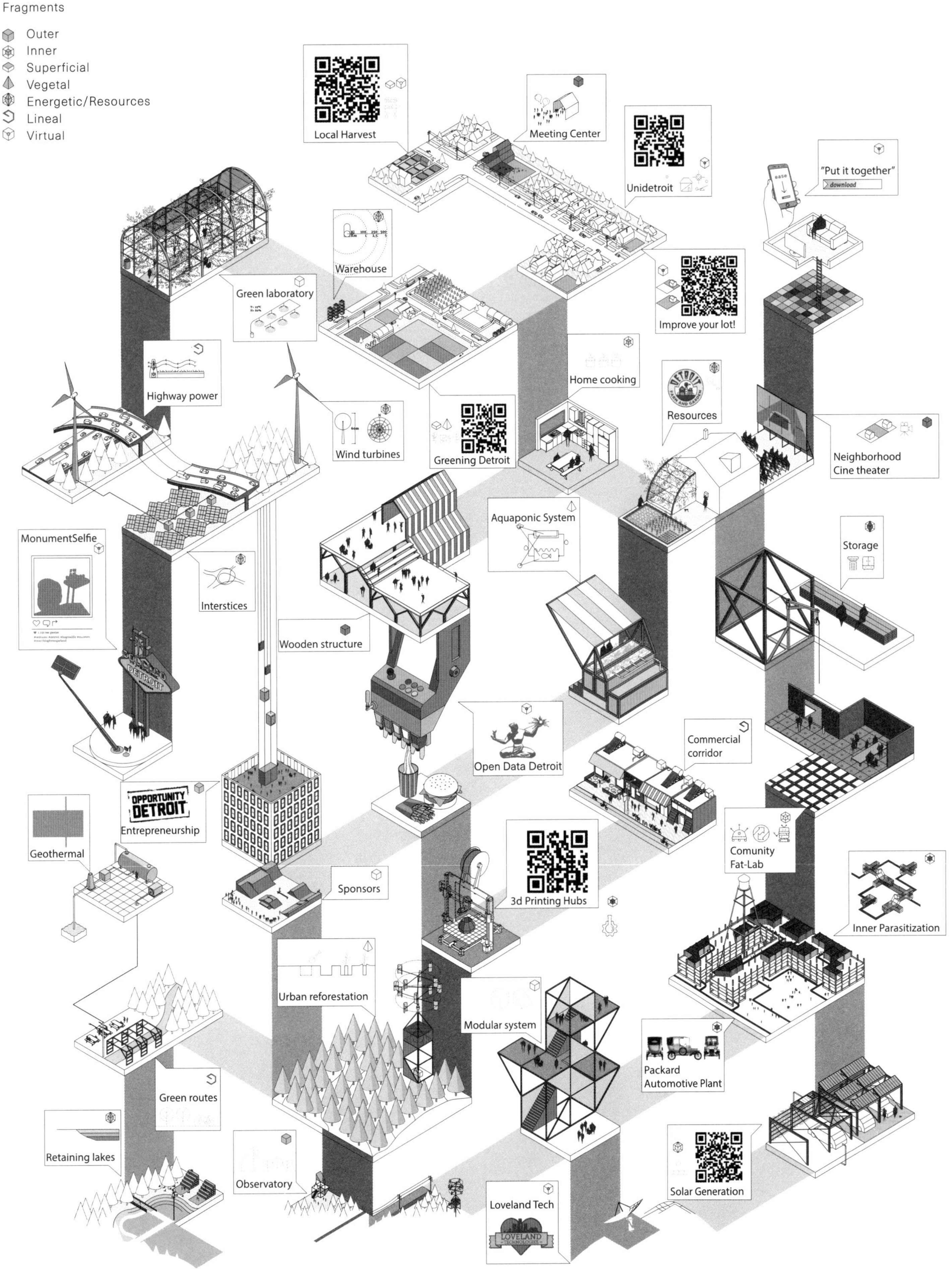
Fragments
Outer
Inner
Superficial
Vegetal
Energetic/Resources
Lineal
Virtual
Local Harvest
Meeting Center
Unidetroit
"Put it together"
download
Warehouse
Green laboratory
Improve your lot!
Highway power
Wind turbines
Greening Detroit
Home cooking
Resources
Neighborhood
Cine theater
MonumentSelfie
Interstices
Wooden structure
Aquaponic System
Storage
DETROIT
Open Data Detroit
Commercial
corridor
OPPORTUNITY
DETROIT
Entrepreneurship
Geothermal
3d Printing Hubs
Comunity
Fat-Lab
Sponsors
Inner Parasitization
Urban reforestation
Modular system
Packard
Automotive Plant
Green routes
Retaining lakes
Observatory
Loveland Tech
LOVELAND
Solar Generation

In Detroit's historic North End, local studio Akoaki, led by the architect Anya Sirota and the French designer Jean Louis Farges, is working with the Oakland Avenue Urban Farm, founded by Jerry and Billy Hebron, to set up a civic commons site. Detroit Cultivator is a six-acre urban plan with food production, cultural activities, and civic assets, that aim to empower the social and economic fabric of the community. The unique effort is grounded in its respect for cultural heritage and social integrity.

AKOAKI WITH OAKLAND AVENUE URBAN FARM

Detroit Cultivator

The North End was once Detroit's premiere cultural nexus: a predominantly African American neighborhood that attracted emerging artists from across the country and influenced vanguard music, fashion, and style on a global scale. Today, it is difficult to find visual evidence supporting that legacy: Detroit's prolonged economic slump and exuberant blight remediation campaigns have erased many material vestiges of its history. 70% of the building stock of the neighborhood is gone, creating a neo-rural landscape in close proximity to the city center. Average incomes are below the poverty line and the majority of the young are under-employed. The neighborhood is home to a high concentration of politically engaged, culturally active residents. Since Detroit's bankruptcy and ensuing economic resurgence, they have become increasingly wary of the city's unbridled blight remediation and redevelopment policies, which was perceived by many as a threat of cultural erasure.

With the new streetcar M1 Rail connecting the neighborhood to the Downtown Detroit area, speculation is on the upsurge and revitalization efforts are growing. These trends make the advance of the Oakland Avenue Farm project critical to equitable local redevelopment, while providing a new way forward for similarly-challenged neighborhoods, nationwide.

For the past decade, the Oakland Avenue Urban Farm—the first 'Agri-Cultural' urban landscape in Detroit's North End—has established its reputation as a stabilizing anchor for the community by growing healthy food, offering mentorships, conducting educational programs, supporting outdoor gatherings, and art spaces. From one lot in the year 2000 to an actual six-acre urban plan, Oakland Avenue Urban Farm regroups thirty lots and eight structures, including public amenities: a civic program, residential accommodations, and architectural systems that contribute to environment sustainability. The productive agricultural landscape is planted throughout the six-acre site, inviting visitors and gardeners to interact directly with the farm's growing beds and orchards. Natural landscapes are also important for the Oakland Avenue Urban Farm: it supports biodiversity, native ecology, and sustainable water management strategies into its long-term vision. The plan is engaging and demonstrative: an educational landscape for all.

Akoaki's work is a successful demonstration of an interdisciplinary project with community commitment that engages special, social, and material realities. Applying tools of design and architecture to convey strong ideas and embody physical needs, their work is constantly exposed to the public and updated in order to push back against gentrification and incorporate current needs and new programs. With its broad network of community and institutional partnerships, the project is sustainable and stands as a living laboratory for practices on an international level.

The North End's challenging socio-economic scenario offers the impetus, space, and opportunity to explore new methods of stewardship, demonstrating that collective work is a key word to reactivate a locally rooted economy.

DATE: 2017 / LOCATION: North End, Detroit, Michigan / STATUS: Completed / DESIGN TEAM: Anya Sirota and Jean Louis Farges in collaboration with Jerry and Billy Hebron / COLLABORATORS: Christophe Ponceau (Landscape Architect), Taylor Montgomery, Sam Okolita, Matthew Story and Annelise Heeringa (Project Team), Arvinder Singh, Rafael Kopper, Sabrina Herbosa Reyes, Alix Eoche-duval / IMAGES: Courtesy of Akoaki. akoaki.com / oaklandurbanfarm.org

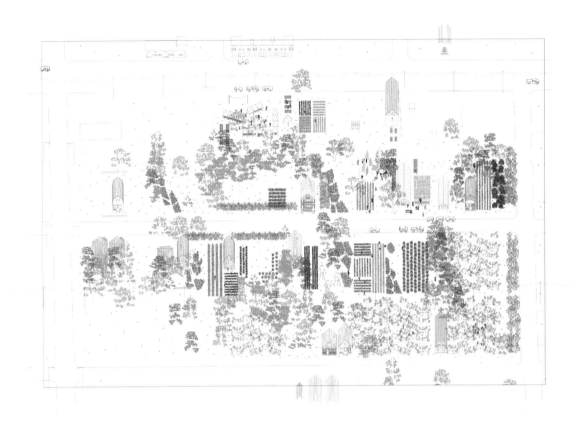

1 Market Row: The first new business construction in decades.

2 The historic Red's Jazz Shoe Shine Parlor

3 The former grocery store at 9400 Oakland Avenue: Non-profit/private partnership between Oakland Avenue Urban Farm and Fellow Citizen, LLC.

4 The Landing: Mid-sized hostel and gastronomic performance center.

5 The UNESCO City of Design Library

6 Ideal Studio: Experimental art center for the exploration of identiy.

7 The Herbarium: Education and retail facility.

8 The Incubator: Hosts the Farm's start-up businesses, providing space, offices, meeting rooms, and retail space featuring value-added products.

9 Water Shed: Market stalls and tool sheds that integrate water-catchment systems.

10 The Farm: Community Center.

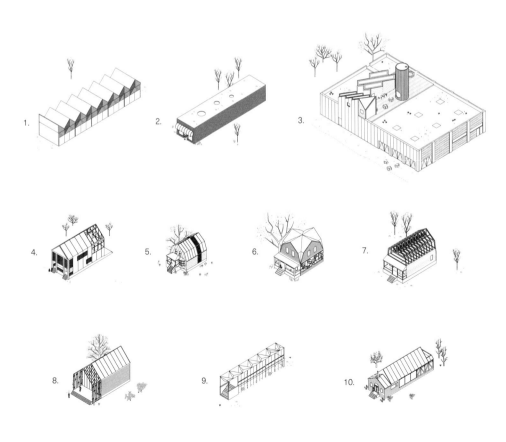

"Well I've said it now / Nothing's changed / People are burnin' for pocket change / And creative minds are lazy / The big three killed your baby / The big three killed my baby / No money in my hand again / The big three killed my baby / Nobody's comin' home again / And my baby's my common sense /

So don't feed me planned obsolescence / Yeah my baby's my common sense / So don't feed me planned obsolescence" *

* From "The Big Three Killed my Baby" lyrics, The White Stripes, 1999.
The White Stripes were a rock duo formed by Jack and Megan White. They played from
1997 to 2011 and are part of Detroit's long and outstanding music tradition.

Along with the public efforts accounted by Maurice Cox and Steven Lewis, many Detroiters have helped to push forward and reinvent the Motor City. Third Man Records and Shinola are examples of two well-known enterprises that have already seen some economic impact while generating nationwide visibility. Their efforts may not be enough to make widespread social change on their own, but they are creating jobs, and boosting gentrification and tourism in certain downtown areas.
Urban farms, entrepreneurship, technological start-ups, and other more neighborly initiatives might be less celebrated abroad, but they are dreaming about a new Detroit, and are essential to the making of a new era.

BETWEEN COZY HISTORY & HOMEY TECHNICS*

Conversations on discursive refuges and projection tools for architecture. Rustically recorded but fully committed.

* We use 'technic' as the performance of technology or arts, specifically when referring to the application of technological issues and processes in daily life.

This section bravely questions architects and thinkers about the intellectual and pragmatic set of tools at hand: Stan Allen & Jesus Vassallo discuss photography and its role in documenting architecture, and the built environment as a filter of abstraction; Enrique Ramirez & Mimi Zeiger reflect on the aesthetics—or lack thereof—in contemporary representation technics; Emanuel Christ & Camilo Restrepo imagine the type as a vehicle for ideas to travel through building cultures; and Sharon Johnston & Florencia Rodriguez exchange views on curating in architecture. Lastly, the idea of the event as a refuge is tested while revising and mapping the biennial phenomenon.

STAN ALLEN &

Realism Re-Presented

STAN ALLEN

I'd like to start by asking about your curatorial project at the Biennial. The title "A Love of the World" implies that architecture is situated not as a separate, autonomous practice but is 'in the world,' and that photography in some ways helps us move between the disciplinary specificity of architecture and this larger question of architecture being embedded in the world.

JESUS VASSALLO

Absolutely, "A Love of the World" is a reference to scholastic philosophy, and to the Bible: "Love not the world, not the things of the world" (1 John 2:15). The title tries to encapsulate an idea of realism as an attack on idealism, but also as an optimistic proposal for the future. This idea of looking at architecture as part of a larger reality as opposed to an isolated abstraction, exactly as you were saying, is quite important for me. I like to think that within the history of architecture there is what I call a realist impulse, which is a recursive thing. It also seems to me that architects who feel this impulse gravitate towards photography as something that enables architecture to make reference to things outside of itself and to engage with the reality of the world around it. I think this condition has to do with the way in which we have come to understand architecture and the built environment as two distinct categories. I have always found this a fascinating thing, that architecture and the built environment—at least in the minds of the architects—are mutually exclusive.

SA

Right. What we usually call architecture is only a small percentage of the built environment, and we need to pay attention to more than that small fraction.

JV

Yes. And, if you think about that problem in art historical terms, it is easy to see some trends. For instance, since the advent of modernism, there has been an anxiety about the political role of art: when new realist practices started to emerge in the postwar period, it was all about this capacity of art, abstract art, to start making references to something outside of itself in order to regain some degree of social relevance. Somehow, the game was to work with a certain abstract language while making references to what we would call vernacular or everyday elements ...That happened in painting, that happened in many other fields. I think that phenomenon was also very related to the idea that in order to be political, art has to become non-art. So, for me, that's fascinating and I think it has been very well discussed in the history of painting and other disciplines, but not so much for architecture. Then the question is: if architecture and the built environment are different things, and if architecture is an artistic discipline which wants to make a reference outside of itself in order to engage in a realist discourse, then, the thing outside of itself is the built environment. This is problematic; how do you make buildings that are about other, less self-conscious buildings? In this context, photography becomes the

tool for architects to approach the built environment already with a certain filter, not only of selection, but also a filter of abstraction. So, in the end, it all comes down to photography having this dual capacity to, on the one hand, allow architects to make reference of the world outside of their immediate disciplinary boundaries, and on the other hand, to work as a first filter of abstraction that enables architecture and its discourse to remain within the realm of form.

SA

What you are saying resonates, for me, specifically with the post-war period in Britain and the Independent Group. If you think of Nigel Henderson and his relationship to the Smithsons, for example. It was very much a way of opening up architecture to the world of the everyday, and in his case, the asphalt city. But today we are living in a very different moment...

JV

Yes, the case between the Smithsons and Henderson is one I like to use as an example of how those relationships change over time. So, for instance, when you look at Venturi and Scott Brown and their fascination with Ed Ruscha just a few years later, that is already something else. I think Ruscha introduces a certain strategy of detachment that hadn't been negotiated by the new realist practices of the European postwar, like Henderson, and his Italian, French or Spanish counterparts. So, I think that's an interesting evolution. Then in the seventies and even later, a

JESUS VASSALLO

sort of shift happens both in architecture and in art and this trend becomes more radical. For instance, I like to compare the relationship of Venturi and Scott Brown with Ruscha's images to the relationship between Herzog and de Meuron and the photography of Thomas Ruff.

SA
Right, very different.

JV
Those two pairs are really parallel in many ways. Both of them deal with issues of superficiality, substantially, and in many ways. And something similar happens if you think about the Smithsons and Henderson and how their influence compares to the relationship of Caruso St John and Thomas Demand; again, both pairs deal with materiality as the defining locus of realism, but in a very transformed way.

SA
They are working also with an awareness of the history of the intervening period—Ruscha in particular because there is a lot of his sense of detachment in Thomas Demand's images. The model and the photograph both distance you from worldly concerns. The world is there, but filtered through flat, deadpan copies. It's interesting because in the earlier examples you described, photography has sort of an evidential value, a truth value. But that self-evident truth value begins to be more ambivalent when you move closer to the present. But I think there's been too much emphasis on the emergence of the digital

as the hinge point: the idea that photography's truth value is undermined because of the manipulability of the photographic image. But I think that what you are saying, and I think it's true, is that it's not actually technology-dependent. It happened long before the widespread availability of digital photography. The doubtfulness of the photographic image is not simply related to digital.

JV
Absolutely. For me the most relevant transformation happens at some point between the mid-sixties and the early seventies. One interesting way to locate the changes in the nature of photographic practices is to compare someone like Walker Evans with Ed Ruscha and then with the New Topographics. Evans is maybe the first documentary photographer who starts to question the humanist component in documentary photography and focuses instead on the idea of an objective visual language as a construct in and of itself. He distinguishes between the use-value of the photographs and the language of photographic objectivity as two different things. The acknowledgement of documentary photography as an explicit visual construct is in a sense opposed to its understanding as a conveyor of truth. Then, that idea, that detachment, is appropriated by Ruscha, not so much in a fully photographic project but for an art practice that is more conceptual and that is making a commentary about art as a whole. Finally, the next generation, including the New Topographics with people

like Bernd and Hilla Becher or Lewis Baltz, re-appropriate the language of objectivity or impersonality for photography as a discipline in an explicit way, but the notion of the transparency of the photograph and the validity of the documentary archiving of reality have been already complicated.

SA
Then, of course, there are other figures who pose a curatorial dilemma: someone like Cindy Sherman, for example, doesn't consider herself primarily a photographer. She's an artist who works with photography. Going all the way back to her earlier work, there is a sense of staging the image, of using the camera as a device. Photography is not being used in a documentary way at all. It's a tool for the construction of artificial images.

JV
Completely. People like Cindy Sherman or Jeff Wall are a product of precisely those changes, and practices like theirs have been a platform to engage a content that is related to the everyday and the relation between fantasy and the everyday. I think it's very pertinent to the discussion about realism but maybe… I think there's a certain tradition within documentary photography and conceptual work that for me is easier to see in direct conversation with architecture. Another way we could talk about this, however, which you have brought up in the past and that I think is fascinating, is trying to understand how different representational techniques become more prominent within architecture

during different periods. You have talked about how in the seventies and the eighties painting was a privileged representational practice for architects. Then, there was the period of the digital explosion that generated another way to represent architecture, and the rendering came out of that. And now there's a photographic emphasis, I would say, which is again a product of a realist emphasis.

SA

I think that's correct, but the return to photography, as you have pointed out, is working under a certain shadow of doubt that is already there in the photographic practices...

JV

In the catalog for the biennial I try to sort out some of these problems. I try to explain that in early modern architecture, abstraction was not considered a monolithic phenomenon: it had different natures, and meant different things for its protagonists. If you think of someone like Gropius, his architecture school was staffed with avant-garde visual artists, but he was also a man who collected photographs of grain elevators and silos. Same thing with Le Corbusier, who was an abstract painter, but who was also obsessed with saw-tooth roofs, zinc bars, and metal sinks. Mendelsohn, I think, offers the best example. He has this book, "Russland, Europa, Amerika", where basically the argument he is making is that modern architecture is or should be a European synthesis of Russian pictorial art and American industry. After the war, when modernism emigrates to America and starts to be conveyed from one generation to another through architecture schools, what happens is that this very balanced understanding of the two facets of abstraction, one pictorial or geometric and the other material or constructive, becomes very unbalanced because basically the pictorial part is much easier to convey in an academic setting as modernism becomes an academicism.

SA

It's an interesting reading. And it resonates with my own experience as a student. I studied in the late seventies and early eighties with John Hejduk at Cooper Union, in an atmosphere still marked by Colin Rowe and Robert Slutsky's transpar-

ency article and their readings of cubism and modernist architecture—precisely the pictorial, academic context that you are referring to. Contemporary painting, even postwar painting, was a blind spot on the map. Hejduk used to say that his knowledge of painting ended in 1940. And it was true; Mondrian was the endpoint for Hejduk. It's remarkable to me how late that persisted in architecture. You can argue that Deconstructivism was still working through these ideas of fragmented cubistic space derived from early 20th century abstract painting. By that moment in the eighties, the discourse of painting had moved far beyond that.

JV

And even earlier, I believe. The first Diamond Houses happened around 1965, I think, which is the same year as Ruscha's peak production of photography books. Between 1965 and 1970 the whole art world is basically producing a response against abstract expressionism, and architecture is somehow going in the opposite direction.

SA

Correct. Peter Eisenman refers to Sol Lewitt and conceptual art, but no, you're right; Venturi and Scott Brown would have to be the exception, I think, and it's significant that in "Learning From Las Vegas", photography plays a key role (not to mention the shadow of Ruscha...)

JV

I think it's a very specifically North American phenomenon. If you look at that period between 1965 to 1970, the art and architecture worlds in the United States are sort of passing by each other, moving in different directions. That explains, I think, a lot of things... it explains why some architects in that context somehow feel this urge to engage with the world through photography... Every once in a while, an architect within an environment where abstraction is dominant feels an urge to look out the window and bring some of the formless reality of the world into the drawing board...

SA

I think that is correct, but I would go back to something you said earlier: that what photography provides architecture is a

model of engagement with the world through the filters of 'selection' and 'abstraction.' Abstraction is one way to push back on architecture's insistent identity as material fact. Abstraction in architecture has to be hard won, and in tension with reality as found—it has to produce a new reality, not reproduce the one that is given. For me, it's almost the defining characteristic of architecture as a practice; there are questions of geometry, measure, and interval that are specific to architecture. I am talking about abstraction not as a negative quality, as a product of reduction, but as a positive quality, won out of the hard logic of matter. I like the way that William Gass puts it: "reality is not a matter of fact, it is an achievement." And I don't think its limited to high architecture—I find that quality of hard-won abstraction in certain vernacular architecture as well. In that regard, the shift from painting to photography as a primary point of reference seems significant, particularly under the shadow of doubtfulness that you describe. Both are representational systems, but they have very different protocols. Photography is interesting as a model precisely because it transforms the raw material of the world into a new kind of abstraction.

I think your analysis is an interesting one, and important to remember. And on that note, I worry that the reception of the Biennial is going to be too easily described as a kind of return to postmodernist strategies. What your description points out is that the nature, and the mode of referring to history today, are very, very different. For one thing, they are filtered through the flattened landscape of photographic seeing that is all around us today.

JV

I am not saying that history was not engaged with in a productive way by postmodernism, but in order to recover history effectively, in our own way and in our own time, I think we first have to acknowledge architecture as being part of a larger material culture at any point in time. I don't think that in the end, the engagement of historical forms by postmodern architecture put it any closer to the reality of the world. It was yet another interesting discourse and repository of forms, but it was really quite inert and distant.

V17-02

V16-02

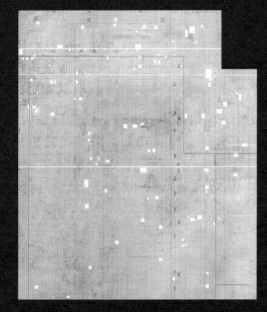

V20-02

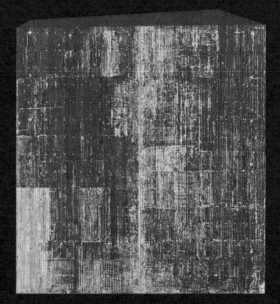

V10-02

Chicago Series, Image Montages by Philipp Schaerer, 2017.

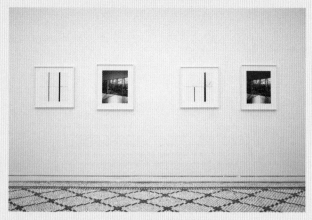

Installation view of Luisa Lambri. Courtesy of Chicago Architecture Biennial, Steve Hall © Hall Merrick Photographers.

"Abstraction in architecture has to be hard won, and in tension with reality as found—it has to produce a new reality, not reproduce the one that is given."

Stan Allen

SA
It was filtered through the screen of signs in the first instance, and the referents were inside the discipline, to historical architectures, and not to the world at large. The linguistic analysis of postmodernism maintained a kind of arm's length relationship with the world through the filter of language. And I think that is very different from the work in the biennial today.

Postmodernism was defined differently in the art world. Arthur Danto's famous declaration of the 'end of art' was in response to Andy Warhol's Brillo Boxes, (and Duchamp before him): the idea that if a fragment of everyday life can be presented in the gallery as art, anything is now permissible. But there was still a level of artifice in Warhol that was erased later with people like Sherrie Levine, who (speaking of Walker Evans), simply appropriated his images. Here I think your point about architecture's necessary relationship to material reality is important: for better or worse, architecture, due to its compromise with constructed reality can never attain the discursive fluidity that you see in some of these art practices.

JV
Absolutely. The language versus image is a fundamental distinction. I think that what we see in this Biennial and very explicitly so on the part of the curators and in my own show is that a recourse to history through images is fundamentally distinct to a recourse to history through language. The immediacy and present-

ness with which photography operates enables a different engagement with historical subject matter which is more direct and more visceral.

Now, on your comment on Warhol and Levine, and the differences between art and architectural production, I think you strike another important point. Architecture cannot operate with the same discursive fluidity as art: its many compromises with reality preclude some modes of operation that are possible in other visual arts. For instance, those art practices experimented with a dissolution of authorship that has been considered problematic for architecture. I think it is really pressing for architects today to reconsider what authorship is, and what degree of authorial voice is necessary or adequate in a work of architecture. It's always a problem when architecture tries to approach the everyday: as a self-conscious discipline, architecture cannot produce unconscious objects. However, I think there is an opportunity today for architects to produce architecture that is a little bit more involved with material culture, or the built environment, through a renewed understanding of what authorship means and basically how much design or how much authorial voice is needed in a given project. How much artifice is needed in order to turn some fragment of the built environment into something more meaningful?

SA
I think that's an important challenge, and one key way to overcome the alienation

that the public so often feels in the face of an architecture that pretends to the avant-garde. One of the things that strikes me about some of the works that you've selected here is that they also seem to be working through architecture's own engagement with material culture. So, they're bringing something to the disembodied medium of photography that comes from architecture as a material practice—it's a two-way exchange.

JV
Yeah, absolutely. The photographers in the show are people primarily from the Fine Arts. They do not have the same preconceptions that we as architects do, and that allows them to redistribute value between high and low modes of architectural production in a more democratic way. You can see that process at work quite actively at the works that both Daniel Everett and Philipp Schaerer produced for the show. I suspect that they understand architecture in a more materialist way than we do, and that is a good thing. The work in the show challenges the notion of modernity as something ahistorical through a material focus, by either producing alternative representations of modernity that open up our understanding of it today, or by approaching the banal urban reality in a way that forces us to enlarge the limits of what we would consider modern, or even architecture.

SA
But even very specifically, there's a consistent use of tight cropping; on the one hand, the close-up view foregrounds tex-

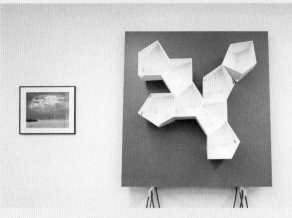

"The immediacy and presentness with which photography operates enables a different engagement with historical subject matter which is more direct and more visceral."

Jesus Vassallo

Installation view of Stan Allen Architect, "The Balloon Frame Revisited", 2017. Courtesy of Chicago Architecture Biennial, Steve Hall © Hall Merrick Photographers.

ture and materiality, but it also carries a strong sense of what the frame excludes. It's more enigmatic; it's never about the expansive overview that would define the architecture as an object, which again belongs to the logic of the rendering. And precisely what annoys me about rendering is that it works with photographic aesthetics but in the most banal and uncritical way possible. That seems like a very conscious choice on your part, to emphasize framing and cropping in this way.

JV
That is a very perceptive point... I had not thought about it that way, but you are very right. I think it may have to do with a little bit of an obsession of mine to think of architecture through its materials. In a very direct way, I see construction materials as a vessel for meaning or knowledge in architecture. For instance, the work of Veronika Kellndorfer is very interesting. She photographs the New National Gallery in

Berlin while it's being rebuilt. You see the old materials being removed and the new materials waiting in stacks. The building is empty, there is no one. The building is like pure matter. She also photographs it along the lines of the curtain wall; then, she prints the images on very large pieces of glass that are roughly the size of the actual glass panels, and that have a materiality in themselves as well. This recourse to material is helpful, for me at least as an architect, in order to think of architecture as a more democratic system. That is also why I like your "Chicago Frame" project so much: that emphasis on a specific material and technology is a non-demagogic way to engage with a wider public, precisely because it deals with architecture as material culture. In Rem Koolhaas's Biennial, for instance, there was an attempt to do something similar, to take basic elements of architecture and say, "a door is a door": everyone has a relationship to doors and it's a very rich thing that we can

all talk about. Marianne Mueller, another artist in the show, has worked at length and in very compelling ways on that topic.

SA
And Luisa Lambri?

JV
Yes, she is another good example, with her fixation on details both in the Farnsworth House and in Crown Hall, she deploys abstraction in order to equalize these iconic buildings with more banal constructions...

SA
Yes, the tightness of cropping the focus on details does that... it's refreshing to think that we can talk about rendering in the past tense.

JV
I think so too! [laughs]

STAN ALLEN is a New York-based architect and Professor of Architecture at Princeton University. From 2002 to 2012 he was Dean of the School of Architecture at Princeton, where he currently directs the Center for Architecture, Urbanism, and Infrastructure. His work has recently appeared in the American Pavilion at the XV Venice Biennale, and at the Chicago Biennial. His architectural work is published in "Points + Lines: Diagrams and Projects for the City" and his essays in "Practice: Architecture, Technique + Representation." "Landform Building: Architecture's New Terrain," was published in 2011, and "Four Projects: A Stan Allen Sourcebook" appeared in 2017.

JESUS VASSALLO is a Spanish architect and writer, and Assistant Professor at Rice University. He is the curator of "A Love of the World," a photography exhibition at the 2017 Chicago Architecture Biennial. Vassallo's work interrogates the problem of realism in architecture through the production of design and scholarship. He is the author of "Seamless: Digital Collage and Dirty Realism in Contemporary Architecture" (Park Books, 2016). His articles and design projects have appeared in several international publications, including AA Files, 2G, Log, Harvard Design Magazine, Domus, and Arquitectura Viva. He has also been an editor of Circo magazine since 2011.

ENRIQUE RAMIREZ

Between the Nest and the Archive: is Architecture at Risk?

ENRIQUE RAMIREZ
Shall we begin with 'Homey Technics' or 'Cozy History'?

MIMI ZEIGER
We get to choose. We can start with either.

ER
My question is: what is the difference? [both laugh] As a historian, I am conditioned to look at technics as an alternative to aesthetics, trying to find a way of understanding the culture of architecture beyond images. But, then again, the question of coziness and hominess requires going back to the culture of images, because they are comfortable, that is, homey and cozy.

MZ
Oh, it's cozy, right? When you put a search filter on it, you know what you're going to get out of it.

ER
Exactly. Instagram is a refuge. Call it a space of refuge.

MZ
Yeah. It is a cozy technic, right? I believe that when we exchange images these days, it isn't about shooting off a roll of film and then disposing of all the bad ones and picking only the good ones. We're only after the good. That's why filters are interesting: they allow us to take something and manipulate it rather than having to sift through pictures that are fuzzy or wobbly.

ER
As an Instagram user, I can make my pictures more distributable, more shareable. You do it, so do I. We alter images to show the limits of the possible. But then again, that's why Instagram is cozy and homey. We do with it as we like.

MZ
So, let's talk more about spaces of refuge and homey technics. When I think of 'homey' I think of phrases like 'someone only a mother can love' or even 'homie' in Latino L.A. gang speak. It reminds me of a Smiths-Morrissey tribute band here called Sweet and Tender Hooligans. They basically take Smiths and Morrissey songs and play them to a mostly Latino group of fans. It's incredible. It's total control over an aesthetic.

Now going back to homey technics, to refuge, I note how stuff like fabrication, computation, Object-Oriented Theory (OOO) are all arriving at an aesthetic that has no control over the aesthetic because it has the ability to proliferate on its own. We need it more than it needs us. Does that make sense?

ER
Don't stop making sense.

MZ
I won't. So back to fabrication, OOO, etc. You don't have to argue or advocate for it because the issue of authorship has become very blurry. You're a historian, which means that you pull stuff out of an archive,

or out of Google Image Search, whatever, in a very flattened way. Authorship then becomes about re-arranging or re-combining rather than creating. It runs against the idea of authenticity or originality. In time, architecture may follow suit and totally avoid any kind of heroic gesture. So maybe we seek refuge from that.

ER
Or it could be the opposite because relinquishing control can be liberating. Being homey or cozy is a kind of relinquishing of control, the technics of comfort and security. For example, do you remember James Bridle and "The New Aesthetic"? If we valorize the glitch, then we don't have to worry about a lot of thinking that may require us to ask why the glitch happened in the first place. You know what I'm talking about?

MZ
Yes. I totally know what you're talking about.

ER
So about being a historian. I confess that I have an archive allergy. Not because I don't find them useful but rather because visiting an archive can be like being inside a sanitized environment or sensory deprivation tank. This too is both homey and cozy, because it's easy to portray the hard work of history as 'finding' something. Finding something becomes the end, not questioning why it's there in the first place or the parameters or provenances of the actual archive. Sometimes we go to the archives because we want something else to do the thinking for us, not because

MIMI ZEIGER

we are really interested how something happened. We accept the evidence as it is and move forward. The same applies to the glitch. "Oh, the glitch!" "Look at this glitchy drone footage, isn't it cool?"

MZ
But the glitch doesn't qualify as a new mode of representation, and yet it is accepted as novel. Same applies to the way Instagram feeds from architecture school have so many projects rendered in pastels and relying on isometric or axonometric projections. What was once a critical mode is now a kind of filter, a tool to make images, and it is no longer beholden to any spatial consequence. Thinking more about cozy history reminds me of the nesting that was happening after 9/11. There was a rise in craft, in D.I.Y. making, in home cooking after the fall of the Twin Towers. Nesting was an inward turn, one that focused mainly on the individual. We can say that something similar happens with the archive, no? In other words, we won't get anything more out of it other than what we've already put into it, right? In that way, it's kind of like the technical, data in-data out, but you are looking in both cases for the reflection of yourself through a sort of pre-authored thesis.

ER
I wonder. In 2017, knowledge about isometrics and axonometrics seem to come mainly out of social media. We hardly mention how this kind of image-making came out of the engineering tradition, of how architects used it to better under-stand objects in three-dimensional space, and especially of how an axonometric is democratizing because it does not privilege elevation over plan or plan over elevation. Now, the axonometric projection is confused for the thing itself. The designer is no longer an author, but a hashtag.

MZ
It goes back to proper nouns, right? The proper noun of authorship, the proper noun of the venue allows us to give legitimacy to something rather than to really look at it. In that sense, it is a continuation of the postmodern tradition, but not necessarily the postmodern tradition that I think we are in at this moment.

ER
Let's talk about the second because the postmodern that is being celebrated right now in biennials is not postmodernism, right? It's part of an insular image culture that does not seem to confront or question some of the ideas that postmodernism tried to flesh out.

MZ
Yeah, because in part, postmodernism as an architectural event was really late to the party. Philosophy, literature, and the fine arts got there first.

ER
In some instances, they were there centuries ago.

MZ
That work of postmodernism as a critique of the after-effects of modernism wasn't always about image. It was about communication, if we consider Venturi and Scott Brown. Postmodernism was about trying to bring about meanings in new ways or explore the fact that there could be meaning in the first place. We are inundated in this image culture; how do we create work that then calls attention to itself as a critique of that very culture that it is in? Is there any hope there? It's not lost on this generation. There's either some really deep irony going on between certain practitioners or it isn't there at all. Or maybe I'm just not getting it.

ER
No need to be alarmist. I don't think architecture culture is dying. Maybe it's that, in its current manifestation, images are so abundant that they are like anodynes. Now I don't want to sound like the old guy scolding kids, but practitioners from before knew what was at stake when they were borrowing from other designers, from history.

MZ
That goes to the question of generations that we've also been talking about. Our generation is the worst when it comes to irony; we've misinterpreted irony. It's not that there isn't humor within the work because I think there certainly is, but it's not aligned with the irony that came from the slacker generation. You see it in the works of the more emerging practices, those that are more generationally aligned with where we are, like MOS or Keith Krumweide. Their

understanding of the postmodern is much more akin to our shared understanding irony and with it a search for meaning and willingness to poke holes in our own pre-conceptions.

ER
Michael, Keith, you, me: we are all roughly the same age.

MZ
We are all middle-aged and dealing with it. I'm glad we are getting that in print. [laughs]

ER
Let's get back to irony and the current condition. One thing that concerns me is that perhaps we are unable to react to the lightning-fast pace of image production. Or the reaction is too tacit, too knee-jerk, and not thoughtful? We're both music fans, so let's go there for a moment. Look at Japandroids' album, "Post-Nothing." What's 'post' about it? What is it reacting to? Are Japandroids postmodern? Post-critical? They're post-nothing. There's nothing. But I love this album cover because it mimics the cover of Television's "Marquee Moon". It's as if the two members of Japandroids are making a sly dig at Robert Mapplethorpe's now iconic cover image. The cover to "Marquee Moon" is one of those images that captures the energy and ennui we associate with the punk scene in seventies New York. This is totally gone from Japandroids' "Post-Nothing". This testament of youth so brilliantly captured by Mapplethorpe has been neutralized. But then again, other album covers seem to show how

designers are able to look back at sources from history and do something interesting with them. Take Peter Saville's sleeve art for New Order's "Power, Corruption & Lies." The cover image is actually a reproduction of an 1890 still life by Fantin-Latour, which Saville then crops and adds his own color alpha-numeric typographic symbols, and then in 2009, Michael Zahn reproduces a jpeg of a close-up of the album cover and replicates it on canvas, and then hangs it in a gallery. I find it so intriguing a proposition because here you have various image cultures colliding and commenting on each other via different media. We need more of this, this sense of play that looks backwards and forwards at the same time.

MZ
It's on the threshold of something.

ER
Precisely, on the threshold. But what does it mean to have a threshold in contemporary architectural culture? What exactly is being crossed?

MZ
That's the question. Maybe this is very cynical of me, but the thresholds of contemporary architectural culture are thresholds of acknowledgment. There's the threshold of getting published, of getting into a biennial, an exhibition, a tenure-track position. These thresholds are the institutional parameters of architectural culture. There's no risk in these other kinds of thresholds, right? Maybe we need to start talking about that it means to the threshold of failure, to 'ride the whirlwind' like Peter O'Toole in "Lawrence of Arabia." This is not comfortable. This is not cozy.

ER
Right. It reminds of the difference between a bungee jumper and Joe Kittinger's leap from a balloon at 103,000 feet. You've seen the images of this, right? They're amazing. Here you see this guy, kind of dressed like a pilot or astronaut, literally leaping into a giant blue-white void. There was so much risk and danger involved. Moving one way during free-fall could result in an uncontrollable spin that would make you unconscious. So many variables, so many chances for grave injury. Not so with bungee jumping. You do it, and though it may be scary, you know that the cord is

not going to snap. Maybe you will get your head wet once you reach bottom, but then you'll have a beer afterwards and tell your friends that it was cool to cheat death. You've cheated nothing. It was done on the fly, but it was always safe. Now with Kittinger jumping from 103,000 feet? There were preparations. There were precautions. But it was never safe.

MZ
But you just had to do it. Henry Rollins—punk icon, former Black Flag member, and now KCRW DJ—was on the radio the other night talking about Jello Biafra—former Dead Kennedys lead singer, songwriter, and activist—and his crazy fearlessness back in the day. He told a story about how the two of them were riding around Los Angeles in the back of a pick-up truck and Jello would make faces at the people in the cars. In a sprawling place like L.A., where every neighborhood comes with a different political frequency, he was trying to piss people off, to shake them out of their comfort zone. He was provoking risk; he was not only taking a risk but he was inciting something to happen, knowing so well that making a face could be really hysterical and potentially very dangerous. Without advocating for danger for dangers sake, how do we raise the stakes a little higher? My argument lately is: we are in a cultural condition that requires that we take a position outside of the discipline. We can't be afraid of crossing that threshold. If we can do that, we may fail but we can also do something super awesome and maybe we can find meaning in taking on issues that seem sort of extra-architectural, like questions of politics, for instance.

ER
I think we're still formulating the stakes of architecture in abstract ways. But let's go there. For example, we can say, "hey, architecture, it's been centuries and you're still not making the impact that artists, writers, or musicians are making, why is that?" Why is it that even though architects have more amazing ways of communicating and distributing work than ever, why does it seem as if the situation has not changed? Are other disciplines always going to be ahead of you in terms of engaging with current dialogues or political developments? This begs the ques-

"Marquee Moon"
by Television. Elektra, 1977.
Ph. Mariam Samur

tion that if other disciplines are always going to be ahead of architecture, what does it mean to be behind? Will it forever be reactive and not proactive? If architecture accepts this, then at what cost?

MZ
The cost is giving up on the idea that architecture must always be new or progressive. To accept that we're operating on the drift or the drag. We're late. And we've always been late. You know you're not going to be the avant-garde, let's stop talking about being avant-garde.

ER
Yes, if we're talking about avant-gardism as a way of political engagement, then that's totally off the table.

MZ
But in this tardy space, there are ways to find allies with the table bussers, the cleanup crews. [laughs]

ER
Right. Look at the images from aerodynamic or hydrodynamic testing. You always see

buffeting and turbulence at the back. That seems like a good place to be.

MZ
That works well with the theory of the long tail—the idea that in culture, marketing, economics, everything is niche, the curve on the graph is flat. Huge market share isn't necessary, just enough hits to stay in the game. But imagine creating turbulence within the long tail, to shout from the back of the room. In a way, we are moving in small circles because it is safer, which is charming and speaks to the ease of coziness, but maybe we should be uncomfortable. Clearly, what is going on throughout culture and politics right now is fraught and twitchy.

ER
It reminds me of how we were all rolling and yo-yoing at the Chicago Architecture Biennial, asking the hard questions, like: "Are we going to the Columbia party or are we just going to hang out at the Athletic Club and drink?"

MZ
We were pretty comfortable doing that.

ER
That's the thing, right? [laughs] There was a kind of a local misbehavior: "I'm not going to go to that thing where everybody else is going."

MZ
Maybe there needs to be more of the "I'm gonna go do my thing over here." I really appreciate the Architecture Lobby, who actually are putting themselves out there to try to make some noise, to try to start a particular conversation. Everybody is institutionally embedded at this point in time, that's how the cultural stuff of it all works, but I would like to believe it is still

possible to make the choice to carve out your own space even though you know you're within a culture that wants you to conform. That's the part of acting out.

ER
I think the Architecture Lobby is a good example. When I met them in Chicago, I didn't realize just how many members they had. It's an organization that hides or lurks within more familiar institutions. I saw former students, and when they told me that they were affiliated with the Architecture Lobby, my initial question was, "now, how many of you are there?" The Architecture Lobby walks among us. Now, suppose you work for whomever by day, and work with the Architecture Lobby at all other times—is this the model of engagement that awaits us, of embedded engagement? I do it. You have to.

MZ
Oh yeah. We all have to.

ER
Have we actually thought about this not as a model of labor but of a theory of the current condition?

MZ
The ability to hold two opposing thoughts in one's mind? Isn't that what empathy and complexity is all about? The empathetic is something that we are missing right now in culture. I don't mean just social empathy. How do you begin to understand an idea that is different from your own while still holding on to your own position? Perhaps with empathy, by understanding that other, you can be more free with your own ideas, you can relax the rigidness of your own positionality. That's the question of stakes, right? You force yourself to take a particular lead—with the hope, trust, that other people will take other leads.

ENRIQUE RAMIREZ is a scholar and historian of modern and contemporary architecture and urbanism. He is working on a manuscript that considers how exchanges between architectural and aeronautical cultures in 18th and 19th century France constructed new, modernized ideas about air and the natural environment.

MIMI ZEIGER is a Los Angeles-based critic, editor, curator, and educator. She is co-curator of the 2018 U.S. Pavilion at the Venice Architecture Biennale. She has curated, contributed to, and collaborated on projects that have been exhibited at the Art Institute of Chicago, the 2012 Venice Architecture Biennale, The New Museum, the Storefront for Art and Architecture, pinkcomma gallery, and the AA School. She co-curated "Now, There: Scenes from the Post-Geographic City," which received the Bronze Dragon award at the 2015 Bi-City Biennale of Urbanism/Architecture, Shenzhen. She teaches in the Media Design Practices MFA program at Art Center College of Design in Pasadena.

EMANUEL CHRIST

Vernacular versus Type:
on Swissness and Colombianness

CAMILO RESTREPO
A couple of years ago, while you were teaching with Christoph at the ETH, you produced this wonderful series of texts on typology published by Park Books. In one of those volumes, the first one, you made a re-edition of Moneo's text. I would like to begin from there.

EMANUEL CHRIST
Interesting to launch from Moneo! It is a very general topic.

CR
Yes, I was thinking about Moneo because of two things. First, his obsession with going deep into the theory of disciplinary conditions. In this case, his obsession with the type forty years ago, when he wrote the text. And secondly, he's been able to push together the technique in a very clear tradition of Spanish architecture that profiles or creates an architect that is rather similar, I would say, to a Swiss architect, or perhaps to a certain generation of Colombian or Latin American architects, where we were concerned about not only operating within the disciplinary boundaries of theory and history but, at the same time, making it possible—or at least visible, verifiable—within a construction in itself. You can visit the place and experience the construction; the theoretical space transforms into a built experience that you can verify. That's why I was thinking about Moneo, and also because of your book, about typology. Immediately your museum in Basel came to my mind, where the floor plan is very beautiful. It

articulates time as typology and, at the same time, you add something new to the typology when you twist the two volumes and they not only appear to be referring to the type as a social, historical organization that went through time, but also, you add one more layer, trying to update that type and making a clear condition of what it is to be or to make a museum today. I guess that Moneo makes for a nice entry point for our discussion.

EC
I totally agree, and I think that it's a very nice starting point. The way you phrase it couldn't be more precise. What I might add is that it is the belief in the reality of the city that gives Moneo's work its orientation, as well as to our work, and I think to yours as well. Meaning that, speaking of history and theory, on the one hand, and technique, on the other, it all comes together in what you call 'experiencing the story of architecture' within a given place. This is what Moneo is about, not only in his texts but also in his work. Ultimately, I understand it as working with open conditions. That's also our understanding of how we should push the profession forward. That is maybe also an interesting question when looking at the Chicago Architecture Biennial. To what extent is history becoming relevant for today's production in relation to the city?

CR
I think that what you're proposing is very nice: how the typology connects with the city. Then it takes us not only to the ques-

tion of how the type forges, or creates a particular relation of architecture with the city, but also how the city is made by these layers of previous or particular organizations. Those are temporary, in the sense that the type creates a temporary organization of space, a temporary organization of architecture but, at the same time, refers to the building itself. It's only possible to make it happen out of the theoretical question, when does it become part of the city, or how do these typologies also shape the city, in the sense that it's possible to be there, it's possible to experience it. I'm very emphatic about the experience because, for many years, I guess, history claimed typology as a very interesting question, but, for many, it was detached from the reality of creating a city.

EC
Yes, I totally agree.

CR
In that sense, I would say that, in the case of your work, this typology makes a connection to history that I find very beautiful. This is also true of the tower you made for the Chicago Architecture Biennial, which is the absolute essence of type, but also the epitome of how a building is placed—creating a lot of possibilities but within a type that is extremely precise. This condition of the specific, which I find so appealing, is very well expressed in that work. The idea of history is very precise in your work and, just to add a little pepper here, I would say that in our case, when working about history or trying to work with

CAMILO RESTREPO

history from Colombia, history becomes evasive in the sense that we need to create our own narratives; in the case of Colombia, we don't have any historical layering of architecture because everything gets demolished pretty much every forty years. This idea of history must be taken out, as if the history of architecture was an open book, no matter where it comes from. Then, you can even freely interpret it and create your own narrative, your own 'new history' somehow. I know there is a kind of danger in doing that because it becomes extremely self-referential, but I'll say that it leaves you with no other possibilities when you don't have a heritage. I don't know; that's complicated, it's what comes to my mind...

EC

Your point sounds very coherent to me. What about your work in Colombia? Speaking of the notion of history or the notion of time, memory and heritage would ultimately lead us to the vernacular. How do you refer to that and to what extent can it still inform your work? Regarding history, you would probably say that there's not much left, there's nothing to build on because it's very temporary compared to other places. It's built, it disappears, it's demolished, so we have to create our own 'new history' in order to be able to create architecture, ultimately. Thinking of 'making new history,' of course, from the moment on that we consider ourselves making history, it is always a new history by definition. What are your techniques in 'making new history'?

CR

I would say that our technics are very irresponsible and conscious at the same time. It is a system for collaging times and appreciations. We use the project as a language, or even a system, to connect times and conditions that perhaps previously made no sense. For instance, you briefly mentioned the idea of the vernacular and—I guess—that's the only thing left, in our case. This vernacularism is very intelligent and very beautiful. But then if we would say that we take vernacular architecture as a reference to build on top of, then we will have to fight another condition, which will be the cliché of Latin American architecture. Then, everybody would expect from Latin America that either the architecture is extremely driven by social causes, which I think in any case it is and it's not necessary to highlight it to the extent it has been in the media, or you'll have to fight modernity that came from the thirties, twenties, forties; which is also the *cliché* of what to expect from Latin American architecture. In the end, you have to reconcile or put many things together that make sense, or at least appear to make sense, not only as a text but also as built form. Then, the type communicates as something that comes from architecture but belongs to a wider, universal culture. It's quite complicated in that sense. In other words, it is about making sense not only with site-specific or locality issues but also referring and feeding our disciplinary matters, which are not necessarily rooted to one place; they belong more to a universal agreement, pretty much as a social contract.

EC

Maybe yes, but that's also why, after forty years, we are again intrigued by this idea of type because type is, by definition, based on the idea of universality. The type is ultimately not linked or related to a place anymore. Originally it was. We could even question to what extent it is possible to have a type without vernacular. Type is either five hundred years old and evolved, or it is only 25 years old. A type is, in general, very simple, it's something that goes beyond the individual solution. It is something that is repeated, reinterpreted and, in that sense, a type is a concept that belongs to the world of ideas, that can travel. It's vernacular, it evolves and becomes like a general universal good in architecture that architects and city users may experience and reinterpret at different points in time, to respond to similar issues but also to tackle new ones. That's what I find interesting, but of course, the type is abstract and if we go back to the project it will be very specific and very much related to the base, and that's so beautiful. That's how ideas in architecture travel, in the end. Much more than images.

CR

I agree. You mentioned something that raised a question for me immediately. When you mention that the type is abstract—I'm not so sure if the ability of the type is precisely to be extremely ambiguous because it is explicit and abstract at the same time. Allowing us to have this kind of conversation, for instance. Interpreting or giving an interpretation of the type as if it belonged to our common culture, in this case, is as saying that the history of architecture provides us with the most specific elements that, in the end, and through the passage of time, have become fundamentals or principles of the most precise condition of architecture. Type is the possibility of linking and giving value to the vernacular and, at the same time, to feed architecture itself, disregarding time and history. So, how does this beautiful possibility of an open text, of how type works, allow you to travel through time and culture? This I find magnificent.

EC
Absolutely. Thinking about what you presented in Chicago, to what extent is type important in your presentation? Or, in general, in the position that you're presenting?

CR
I would say that, in our case in Chicago, the idea of type is more left open for conversation. We used the engraving of Marc Antoine Laugier, the Primitive Hut, to open the discussion with a question: "What does type refer to?" Because, how do we connect that with the construction of the Farnsworth House where you only see slabs and columns that are connected to vernacular buildings from the 19th Century of the coffee processing areas in Colombia? The same type belongs to two specific conditions: where the slabs and the columns let air go through, and, at the same time, organize and mark the difference between inside and outside. That's how the type manages different conditions. I would say that type is the intermediate condition between time, history, climate, and social organizations. It is what allows us to have a conversation through time, much more than images, as you mentioned before.

EC
I totally agree.

CR
But then of course, when we believe in the technique—not only as a matter to put some tools together to define or create a strategy—we think about a certain approach to materiality that I think is interesting, in your work, and the work in Switzerland, in general. There is this kind of Swissness that you can read, which

again belongs to time, like how materiality connects. It is important and beautiful, your work—and that of your colleagues—take very different approaches, but this idea of Swissness is still readable because there is a certain connection with the technique. I would say that every Swiss architect has this knowledge about material technique, about this condition of having a material expression that articulates in a positive way this idea of type and makes a very big difference, for example, from our condition where we are more constrained. It's not a matter of resources but of skill—I would say—to create this spirit of materiality, as in Switzerland, or Spain even, perhaps also Japan. There is a kind of Swissness, Japaneseness, we could not say that about Colombia ... Colombianness is more about porous spaces, more open, less of an object, perhaps more as a collage, betting on single materials, and more episodic in its reading. A difficult whole ...

EC
Maybe not, I don't know, but what you are describing is interesting. I'm sure you are right, although I cannot see it exactly the same way because, from within, it is a little bit more difficult to have that view on Swiss architecture. We are trying to believe in craftsmanship and there are possibilities to achieve that quality. There still are knowledgeable people who can do that. To a certain extent, in all different cultures you'll find the same thing: in Japan or, as you were saying, in Spain, or Portugal. It has very much to do with the people who build. I don't know how present is craftsmanship in Latin America or in Colombia, for instance. How much professional knowledge is still available? This is what counts and we, Swiss architects, still try to challenge this knowledge to engage with it and to really make it happen. I feel it is totally anachronistic, to be honest. I find it beautiful but I can't get rid of the feeling that this is almost like a lost period of time and that's also what's worrying me a bit, because we cannot base our understanding of architecture on something that seems to be disappearing. At the same time, I have the energy to fight for it but it's a very frustrating thing because you can see how it gets weaker and weaker; also in Switzerland, by the way.

CR
I think you're putting it in an interesting perspective. I never thought about it from that line and when I think about our condition I will say that it is extremely basic in the sense that construction labor is often performed by people with no training or even with no education. Therefore, we need to reduce the complexity or the processes that are involved in the way that we build because otherwise they will all go extremely wrong. If we tried to cast concrete in a Swiss way it would be a disaster because then it will have a lot of flaws that will make it appear to have a very bad finish. It will be more like trying to look like somebody else. So I guess we try to use a certain skill level of this labor to make it a little bit rough, to take advantage of roughness.

EC
I think that the very close relationship I was describing between labor, crafts, and architecture, can also to a certain extent become an intellectual mindset. For instance, what is sometimes described as Swiss—that is, the focus on materiality and perfect finishes—I have to say I find sometimes very boring. We've had the discussion where we were asking ourselves: "How can we get rid of that mediocre obsession with being perfect in terms of finishing, you know?" Because that is also a Swiss/German mentality that is not necessarily interesting, and when I look at our architecture I'm also interested in South America, for instance. There, it can be that you find beautiful, perfect carpentry, windows, wooden windows, all that, but the concrete is, as you were describing, rough and maybe carelessly done and that's the most beautiful thing you can get. In Switzerland, this is almost impossible ... That's an interesting discussion, even though it is a little bit *cliché*, in the sense that we are all looking at other contexts from our normal environment and we see potential. I'll add one more thing that is not very theoretical. It is not necessarily related to type and history, but it might be related to the notion of technique. In Europe, the constraints, restrictions, and obsessions with minimizing risks, which is the same in the United States, take such an important role in architecture that construction and techniques are heavily influenced,

if not dominated by it. That's something which I see as a great challenge. All these constraints and regulations that are swallowing our profession, force us as architects into a paradoxical position that we could call the 'conservative/innovative.' We are conservative because we dream of keeping and maintaining basic qualities, physical qualities, sensual qualities, atmospheric qualities of architecture, but it's almost impossible to still get it that way. In Switzerland, it's almost impossible to do these kinds of trashy things. How can we possibly get there, to that materiality and the immediate physical presence of things?

CR

Yeah. I think that we are reaching a very interesting point of view. I don't know if I will be able to summarize it in a way. Somehow technics have become a kind of Frankenstein which haunts us without any control. Precisely because of the extreme control in the cases of the European Union or the United States where all comes down to regulations, liabilities. All these things reduce the palette for materiality and the technique that we choose. It haunts us like something that has its own life. In the case of Latin America, we get haunted as well by the same ghost 'technics' but precisely from its opposite condition, because of its lack of control or rigor.

The idea of type being somehow autonomous goes against this idea of technics, as we were talking about. This monster, Frankenstein, made out of codes, regulations, liabilities, or made by the lack of it, has a life on its own that we cannot control. Somehow this idea of typology as a condition for having autonomy and the technics being a kind of obstacle that you have to deal with every time to have an approach to an architecture that is possible takes us to a strange and contradictory position: type is restricted in its condition but open as a freedom giver, while technics are apparently open and free for interpretation but become precisely an obstruction. They are, in the end, a crucial player or definer of identity.

EMANUEL CHRIST graduated from the Swiss Federal Institute of Technology (ETH) in 1998. In the same year, he founded the firm Christ & Gantenbein, with Christoph Gantenbein in Basel. Remarkable projects by the office include the extension for the Kunstmuseum in Basel as well as for the Swiss National Museum in Zurich both completed in 2016. Christ has taught and lectured at a number of schools, including ETH Studio Basel (2000–2005), the Accademia di Architettura in Mendrisio (2004, 2006, 2009) the Oslo School of Architecture and Design (2008), as well as the ETH Zurich (2010–2015). He currently teaches at Harvard GSD.

CAMILO RESTREPO OCHOA is an architect graduated from Universidad Pontificia Bolivariana in Medellin in 1998. He was a guest lecturer at Harvard Graduate School of Design from 2014 to 2017 and has been nominated for the MCHAP price in 2014, BSi Prize in 2014, and was one of the three finalists of the Rolex Mentor Protege 2012. In 2010, Restrepo and Juliana Gallego Martínez founded AGENdA (agencia de arquitectura), in Medellín, Colombia.

Interior view, List Customer Center in Arisdorf, 2010 - 2015.
Courtesy of Christ & Gantenbein, Ph. Stefano Graziani.

SHARON JOHNSTON

Uncomfortable Afterthoughts: Continuity, Autonomy, History

FLORENCIA RODRIGUEZ

For this first issue, the subject proposed for The Dossier is related to the biennial and other phenomena of the architectural culture that I've been trying to decode for a while. I am specifically talking about this 'history-comeback' that seems to have gotten so popular in the last years, and, on the other hand, a renewed trust in technics. These two ways of what I would describe almost as a kind of faith seem to be supported by the belief in some fundamental, authentic, and hard knowledge. It really caught my attention … and I've been trying to interpret the causes of this contemporary disciplinary romance, rehearsing different ideas in group discussions, at school with my students, and in certain texts I previously wrote. That's why I got really interested in your statement for the biennial and those ideas of modernism, history, and oppression.[1] I think it can be natural to justify a collective recovery of historical relevance after the complex social processes of the first half of the 20th century for which the modern pioneers needed to declare the obsolescence of the past. But now we truly are in such a different time! So much is juxtaposed, or at least coexisting—some in peaceful simultaneity, others in a terribly conflictive friction. That's why I tend to think that we are not only immersed in a cyclical dialogue but that there is no actual consciousness of the political meaning of this

phenomenon. I want to throw this on the table and ask you, why do you think a very particular and canonical history—to qualify it in a way—is so present? When in the title I implied history as a coziness provider, I'm implicitly suggesting that it might be working as a discipline refuge or even as a trend … Or are we collectively urging the discipline to constitute itself as such again? What do you think about that?

SHARON JOHNSTON

We came to this subject from the perspective of our own practice and observations of a generation of colleagues working around the world. When we began thinking about the biennial and the role of artistic directors, we also thought it was important to reflect on work and themes of the first biennial in Chicago. We wanted to build continuity between the first exhibition and the 2017 program, and perhaps uncover certain ideas that might be picked up in future shows. Especially for such a nascent program, it was essential for us to build upon the ideas of the first biennial, where we saw projects in which history and the contemporary were intertwined in productive ways.

Cozy history is a nice term because we are in an era when imagery and material information is so present and accessible; how we look back, how we engage the past in our contemporary world is very different

today than it was with the most recent and notable return to history of postmodernism. Today there's much more fluidity between how architects are dealing with the past in contemporary discourse, and our understanding of cities today. In the evolution of our discipline there have been certain moments to look inward and take stock of where we are. Participants in the biennial share an interest in engaging with history as a way to operate in contemporary contexts. These architects are not necessarily starting from points of rupture or an obsession with newness as it relates to innovation in a way that generations before us might have. There's an idea about continuity as being almost inherited in the way we think about our work in the contexts in which we build. At the same time, autonomy, as it relates to buildings embodying a level of resistance, is also relevant today.

FR

I like that idea of continuity but I also think that each moment of time in a way conditions which kind of history you look at and how you decide to build on it—whether you do it based on continuity, ruptures, or transculturation, for instance … These are interesting processes …

At the same time, something else that I think is not minor, is that in the last decades we have witnessed many experiences

1 "Today, history represents neither an oppressive past that modernism tried to discard nor a retrograde mind-set against unbridled progress." Excerpt of the statement for the Chicago Architecture Biennial 2017. Available online at chicagoarchitecturebiennial.org/statement

FLORENCIA RODRIGUEZ

of bottom-up urbanism and architecture related to the urgency to respond to the problems attached to density and social injustice. Issues that had been absolutely neglected by architects for a long time. Those cases sometimes messed with the idea of what architecture is or should be. In that sense, I take a risk saying that in this 'history-comeback' (I'm not fully convinced of this terminology and what it implies but I cannot find yet a better way to briefly put it into words), there's something about questioning the intellectual and practical set of tools that architects need to redefine or tend to defend. In a way, I believe it is implicitly pointing out that we shouldn't be talking about the same things that we did decades ago, but better learning from history as a kind of depository that could give us some hints on how to understand where we are and where we could be.

SJ

This has been a topic of discussion that's come out of not only this biennial, but more generally: the role of social practice in architecture, if that's what I understand that you're getting at? We are optimistic about the potential for architecture to embrace social life in the making of cities as positive places, enhancing our shared experience of the built environment. But we also see the limits of what architecture can do, and I think that part of what came out of projects and discussions about the biennial is that sometimes understanding history isn't always about blending in, about reflecting past ideas; it's also about

autonomy, about making breaks, about finding different roles for architecture. Part of what we were trying to ask with the biennial is, what are the boundaries of architecture? How can we bring the discussion back to kind of core disciplinary questions while still looking outward, re-engaging with pressing issues of our time, both recognizing what our tools are and claiming them in ways that are critical for contemporary society?

FR

Yes, I agree to that, and that's what I was thinking when we ran into each other during the opening week and I told you that yours was a brave take, as curators. I was thinking about that in relation to Aravena's position for the past Venice Biennial, which was very much politically right but it also could lead to misinterpretations... As a South American, I'm critical about certain ways of thinking about architecture that can perversely standardize and establish as permanent what I see as emergency solutions that should be temporary. When you deeply analyze some proposals for informal situations that deal with very conflictive social problematics, it is important to be objective about the long-term consequences of what they are dealing with.

That's why I thought that putting this together and pushing some thinking about the specificity of the set of tools and roles that define architecture in an autonomous way can be interesting at this point. So, I could say that I don't agree very much

with the criticism that you have received about the absence of social topics at the biennial and, in fact, some of the participants responded to that in less obvious terms. The case of Tatiana Bilbao inviting other people to participate in her tower is a clear example.

SJ

Yes, Tatiana's project does put forward an interesting example. Another approach to this kind of social practice project was the presentation by 51N4E of their project for Sanderberg Square in Tirana, which looks at new models for designing a public space. This project was formed around a collaboration with the artist Anri Sala. Their presentation, "Personal Histories," presents the experimental process they undertook, which integrated local and international publics and design experts. The presentation, in the form of a salon as a place of discussion, illustrates how they merged layers of spatial, ecological, and empirical research into an ongoing process of storytelling, collaboration, and construction of the square. The stories they collected and mapped built up a deeper understanding, for the designers, of the social importance of this square in the history of the city, and its citizens' hopes for its future. The artist and architect were open to the diverse narratives that informed this place historically, but they have integrated this knowledge into a visionary work of architecture that will be enduring, timeless, and flexible, and not merely a bottom-up agglomeration of wishes.

Installation view of Sylvia Lavin with Erin Besler, Jessica Colangelo and Norman Kelly, "Super Models", 2017. Courtesy of Chicago Architecture Biennial, Steve Hall © Hall Merrick Photographers.

Cover of Plot 31, "¡Oh sí, Posmodernismo!" (Oh yeah, Postmodernism!). In 2016's July issue, Florencia Rodriguez investigates the various forms this 'history-comeback' took in the last years.

FR

Exactly. And in that context, do you think there's something like a 'post-digital time'? I like speculating about how our times will be thought of in the future and I think when you are making the call to 'make new history' you are also trying to generate something. What do you think about that?

SJ

Yeah. I think for sure. I wouldn't say it's an inherent critique. I think that certainly every architect today is using digital tools, but these tools are no longer just an end in and of themselves. "Vertical City" was an interesting barometer. Today, the parameters of contemporary extreme skyscrapers that we're seeing right now in the Middle East and Asia are driven directly by innovations in technology and digital tools of design and production. Alternatively, in "Vertical City," we saw a focus on new material paradigms, an enduring interest in type, and a search for continuities between the tower with that of the surrounding urban fabric through new ideas about the role of the structure and infrastructure in tall buildings and possibilities for collective social space.

FR

That's interesting. And this is just personal curiosity as a curator myself, do you have a favorite installation at the biennial?

SJ

"Vertical City," as a collective, was a powerful project for us. With each of the fifteen architects responding to the same prompt and the historical narrative of the Chicago Tribune Tower Competition, first from 1922, and followed by the 1980 redo, we have presented a spectrum of interests and concerns coming from contemporary global practices. The conception of this project also emerged from our desire to engage this great room of Yates Hall, the former reading room within the Chicago Public Library, for which this historic building was originally designed to house. Walking through this beautiful room, immersed within these tall towers as a hypo-style hall, creates a new spatial dynamic to contemplate these ideas about the future of tall buildings, all the while the historic skyline of Chicago is just outside the windows. When we were questioning whether we should do this project, we thought—why do another biennial, what's the point? So much information is instantaneously available and new biennial programs are starting every year. As a response to this challenge, we wanted the exhibition to engage the architecture of the Cultural Center in meaningful ways, to invite audiences into new spatial environments. Our program engages the city of Chicago and its history, which offers opportunities to embrace new audiences that have come to the city to explore the Chicago architecture. I think that was part of our mandate.

We are also pleased with the contributions that artists made to the show. Jesus Vassallo curated a show within the exhibition entitled "A Love of the World," which

is on view throughout the building and in satellite sites. Some of these projects include commissions to create contemporary portraits of canonical buildings of this region through the personal lens of these artists. The artists have captured more ephemeral or invisible qualities of architecture. Luisa Lambri created a new suite of images of Mies' Farnworth House and Crown Hall, which as a series unveils the subtle atmospheres and materials of these buildings. Jim Welling's images of Mies, processed with contemporary software filters, reveal how the passage of time marks these icons that still dominate the urban skyline of Chicago.

FR

I read something you said in a previous interview about your own practice, in which you sustained that you were not interested in showing during which period of time your buildings were completed. Did I get that well? I think it is a powerful yet subtle idea.

SJ

Aspects of time and transformation are qualities embodied in the work of many architects in the biennial. While recent critics have used the word 'boring' to describe works in the exhibition, we believe there is a richness and complexity that is discovered over time. We love Ed Ruscha's mantra which favors "huh...wow" versus "wow...huh," which could describe so many flashy iconic buildings of recent decades. Perhaps we were talking about our building for the Menil Drawing Institute. We were fascinated at the outset with understanding the history of the Menil, the family, and Renzo Piano's great building for the Menil Collection. Critics have noted that when our building is finished, perhaps it will be unclear if it came before or after Renzo's building. Being out of time is something that we find to be a powerful quality of architecture that draws you in, but doesn't necessarily situate you at one place or one moment in time. It conveys a perception of presentness and groundedness—ephemerality and weight—contrasting qualities that we find powerful in architecture.

FR
What do you think about technics? Or what does it mean for your practice? Because it's not something that you intend to show off within your projects or buildings.

SJ
In the American context, often our audiences want us to demonstrate what the building does, and I guess for us we are more interested in how it feels to experience our buildings. Architects in America have a predilection to prove the intelligence of the building through drawing or diagramming—the ubiquitous red and blue arrows illustrating hot and cold air flow. For us, qualities of the architecture are more interesting and we don't feel the need to tell you everything about our process. We want you to inhabit our buildings

to understand them. It's an American tendency to demonstrate every step you took to get to the end, which is the finished building. Obviously, we're doing all of the engineering work as well, but we don't feel the need to validate our work through this discourse.

FR
So it's just an intrinsic part of the thing, then. And going back to curating, was it your first time? How do you feel about this experience?

SJ
We've worked on exhibitions before, and curated small gallery shows over the years. When we considered taking on this project, our goal was to create a platform to engage in questions with our colleagues, collaborators, and public audiences. It's not something we may do again, but it was a great opportunity. It gave us a chance to study so many great projects and work with our colleagues in ways that we otherwise would not have had the chance to, which was a pleasure for us and our team. Curating a biennial, versus curating a show of a single architect or artist, is so different. We wanted to create spatial experiences that engaged the Cultural Center but also put the work of different architects in dialogue. When we began placing the work within the rooms of the Cultural Center there was an initial tendency on the part of the architects to

put up walls and have their own pavilion. It was challenging to negotiate that with them but we have enjoyed discovering synergies among projects in collective rooms of the show. In Exhibition Hall, for example, Sylvia Lavin's project, "Super Models," is paired Baukuh and Stefano Grazziani's pavilion, "The Chapel for Scenes of Public Life"—another super model. Baukuh's pavilion relates to DOGMA's "Rooms," which compliments Veronika Kellndorfer's photographs of Mies van der Rohe's Berlin National Gallery, depicted as an empty room in the city as the building undergoes a renovation. For the architects, there was a positive energy around the opening; we took the chance to be together and discuss the work, which we feel very positive about. Some aspects of the show weren't exactly what we expected, but all in all, we think the show sets the stage for the next exhibition in 2019, and now we can officially declare that this is a biennial program!

FR
I really value the idea of not being too comfortable with something when you are working and thinking, usually something more thrilling and unexpected comes out when that happens. And I can imagine that curating this Biennial wasn't cozy or homey at all! [laughs]

SJ
Exactly! [laughs]

SHARON JOHNSTON, F.A.I.A., is a partner of the Los Angeles-based firm Johnston Marklee. Since its establishment in 1998, Johnston Marklee has been recognized nationally and internationally with over 30 major awards. A book on the work of the firm, entitled "HOUSE IS A HOUSE IS A HOUSE IS A HOUSE IS A HOUSE," was published by Birkhauser in 2016. Johnston has taught at the Harvard Graduate School of Design, Princeton University, the University of California, Los Angeles, and has held the Cullinan Chair at Rice University and the Frank Gehry International Chair at the University of Toronto. Together with partner Mark Lee, Johnston was the Artistic Director of the 2017 Chicago Architecture Biennial.

FLORENCIA RODRIGUEZ is an architect, critic, and lecturer. She is one of the founders of Lots of architecture publishers, where she acts as Chair and Editor in Chief. In 2010, Rodriguez founded PLOT, one of the ongoing leading publications in Spanish. In 2013 she received the Loeb Fellowship from the Harvard Graduate School of Design. She teaches Theory at Torcuato Di Tella University in Argentina, and has taught isolated courses in other institutions abroad. She has received awards for her editorial work and acted as juror in various opportunities, among which the Mies Crown Hall Americas Prize stands out.

CELEBRATING ARCHITECTURE

The biennial as a regional, collective, and inconclusive phenomenon

ISABELLA MORETTI

To understand the biennial as a wider cultural object means to reflect on its global network as well as on the emergence (or rather the establishment) of a new mode of practice; to look at its geographic, financial, discursive, and strategic aspects and limitations. Architecture exhibitions are hardly something new, but in light of the recent proliferation of events, what has changed? Are biennials or triennials a medium, a critical project, or a message? Phillip Ursprung suggests that it is "the most dynamic platform of mediation and exchange,"[1] Pedro Gadanho highlights its "potential for new critical possibilities,"[2] while Joseph Grima conceives "the exhibition space as a laboratory."[3] One thing is certain: it is not a disciplinary niche anymore and to treat it as such would be to neglect a major shift in contemporary architecture culture. The biennial is conceptually twofold: it acts on the discipline's discourse as well as on the role architecture plays in society, and how it represents itself to the general public. It is a platform to project, to reframe the present, to make ideas public, to speculate about the future, to share histories, to build utopian or near-future scenarios and reflect upon them. At the same time, it is the place where architecture engages with larger, contextual issues such as politics, ethics, economy, gender, ecology, technology, and so on.

1   Phillip Ursprung in "The End of Theory." Available online at e-flux.com/architecture/history-theory
2   Pedro Gadanho, "Is Curating the New Criticism?" In: "Architecture Beyond Criticism: Expert Judgement and Performance Evaluation". New York: Routledge, 2015.
3   Tom Vandeputte, "Sites of Experimentation: In Conversation with Joseph Grima." In: OASE 88, available online at oasejournal.nl/en/Issues/88

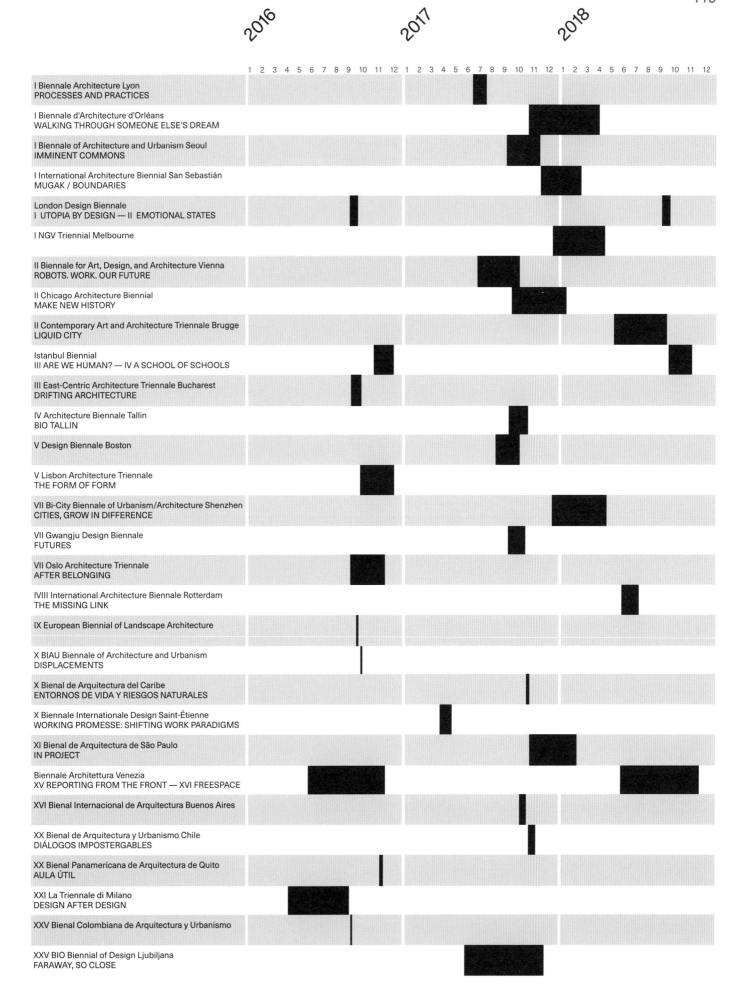

2016   2017   2018

1 2 3 4 5 6 7 8 9 10 11 12   1 2 3 4 5 6 7 8 9 10 11 12   1 2 3 4 5 6 7 8 9 10 11 12

I Biennale Architecture Lyon
PROCESSES AND PRACTICES

I Biennale d'Architecture d'Orléans
WALKING THROUGH SOMEONE ELSE'S DREAM

I Biennale of Architecture and Urbanism Seoul
IMMINENT COMMONS

I International Architecture Biennial San Sebastián
MUGAK / BOUNDARIES

London Design Biennale
I UTOPIA BY DESIGN — II EMOTIONAL STATES

I NGV Triennial Melbourne

II Biennale for Art, Design, and Architecture Vienna
ROBOTS. WORK. OUR FUTURE

II Chicago Architecture Biennial
MAKE NEW HISTORY

II Contemporary Art and Architecture Triennale Brugge
LIQUID CITY

Istanbul Biennial
III ARE WE HUMAN? — IV A SCHOOL OF SCHOOLS

III East-Centric Architecture Triennale Bucharest
DRIFTING ARCHITECTURE

IV Architecture Biennale Tallin
BIO TALLIN

V Design Biennale Boston

V Lisbon Architecture Triennale
THE FORM OF FORM

VII Bi-City Biennale of Urbanism/Architecture Shenzhen
CITIES, GROW IN DIFFERENCE

VII Gwangju Design Biennale
FUTURES

VII Oslo Architecture Triennale
AFTER BELONGING

IVIII International Architecture Biennale Rotterdam
THE MISSING LINK

IX European Biennial of Landscape Architecture

X BIAU Biennale of Architecture and Urbanism
DISPLACEMENTS

X Bienal de Arquitectura del Caribe
ENTORNOS DE VIDA Y RIESGOS NATURALES

X Biennale Internationale Design Saint-Étienne
WORKING PROMESSE: SHIFTING WORK PARADIGMS

XI Bienal de Arquitectura de São Paulo
IN PROJECT

Biennale Architettura Venezia
XV REPORTING FROM THE FRONT — XVI FREESPACE

XVI Bienal Internacional de Arquitectura Buenos Aires

XX Bienal de Arquitectura y Urbanismo Chile
DIÁLOGOS IMPOSTERGABLES

XX Bienal Panamericana de Arquitectura de Quito
AULA ÚTIL

XXI La Triennale di Milano
DESIGN AFTER DESIGN

XXV Bienal Colombiana de Arquitectura y Urbanismo

XXV BIO Biennial of Design Ljubiljana
FARAWAY, SO CLOSE

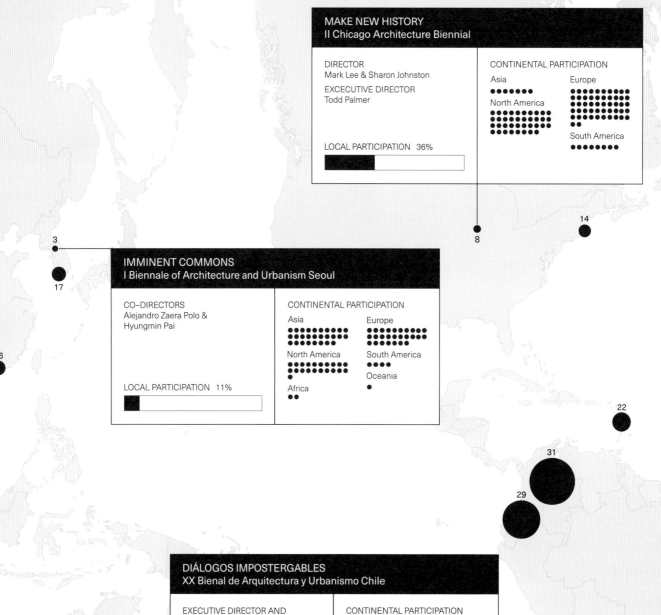

MAKE NEW HISTORY
II Chicago Architecture Biennial

DIRECTOR
Mark Lee & Sharon Johnston

EXECEUTIVE DIRECTOR
Todd Palmer

CONTINENTAL PARTICIPATION

Asia

North America

Europe

South America

LOCAL PARTICIPATION 36%

13

3

17

14

16

IMMINENT COMMONS
I Biennale of Architecture and Urbanism Seoul

CO-DIRECTORS
Alejandro Zaera Polo &
Hyungmin Pai

CONTINENTAL PARTICIPATION

Asia

North America

Africa

Europe

South America

Oceania

LOCAL PARTICIPATION 11%

22

31

29

DIÁLOGOS IMPOSTERGABLES
XX Bienal de Arquitectura y Urbanismo Chile

EXECUTIVE DIRECTOR AND
GENERAL CURATOR
Felipe Vera

CREATIVE DIRECTOR AND CURATOR
OF SPECIAL PROJECTS
Rodrigo Tisi

CONTINENTAL PARTICIPATION

Asia

North America

Africa

Europe

South America

LOCAL PARTICIPATION 53%

28

27

6

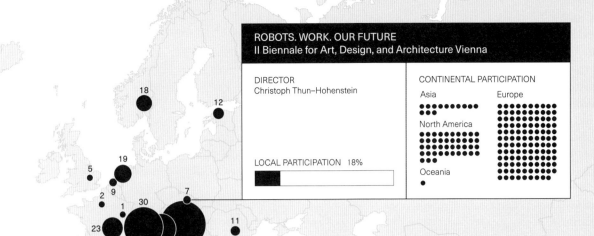

ROBOTS. WORK. OUR FUTURE
II Biennale for Art, Design, and Architecture Vienna

DIRECTOR
Christoph Thun–Hohenstein

CONTINENTAL PARTICIPATION
Asia   Europe

North America

Oceania

LOCAL PARTICIPATION   18%

This map pinpoints 32 biennials or triennials of design or architecture. The scale of the circles increase according to the number of editions each event celebrated. NESS selected four events in quite different locations for in depth analysis in order to compare global and local participation.

1   I Biennale of Architecture Lyon
2   I Biennale d'Architecture d'Orléans
3   I Biennale of Architecture and Urbanism Seoul
4   I International Architecture Biennial Donostia San Sebastián
5   I London Design Biennale
6   I NGV Triennial Melbourne
7   II Biennale for Art, Design, and Architecture Vienna
8   II Chicago Architecture Biennial
9   II Contemporary Art and Architecture Triennale Brugge
10 III Istanbul Design Biennial
11 III East-Centric Architecture Triennale Bucharest
12 IV Architecture Biennale Tallin
13 V China International Architectural Biennial
14 V Design Biennale Boston
15 V Lisbon Architecture Triennale
16 VII Bi-City Biennale of Urbanism/Architecture Shenzhen
17 VII Gwangju Design Biennale
18 VII Oslo Architecture Triennale
19 VIII International Architecture Biennale Rotterdam
20 IX European Biennial of Landscape Architecture
21 X BIAU Biennale of Architecture and Urbanism
22 X Bienal de Arquitectura del Caribe
23 X Biennale Internationale Design Saint-Étienne
24 XI Bienal de Arquitectura de São Paulo
25 XIII BEAU Bienal Española de Arquitectura y Urbanismo
26 XV Biennale Architettura Venezia
27 XVI Bienal Internacional de Arquitectura Buenos Aires
28 XX Bienal de Arquitectura y Urbanismo Chile
29 XX Bienal Panamericana de Arquitectura de Quito
30 XXI La Triennale di Milano
31 XXV Bienal Colombiana de Arquitectura y Urbanismo
32 XXV BIO Biennial of Design Ljubiljana

TRADITION AND LOCATION

First, the facts. In 2016 and 2017, at least ten design or architecture biennials or triennials were launched, of which 80% were in Europe. More than half of the total number of events happen in Europe now but this is only fairly recent. South and Central America evidence a longer biennial habit—an average of sixteen editions which translates to approximately 32 years of tradition. The *Bienal Colombiana de Arquitectura y Urbanismo* in Bogotá, for example, sums ten editions more than the *Biennale Architettura di Venezia*, rendering the Biennial of Design Ljubljana, with its 25 editions, as an isolated event. The events in South America are usually shorter, more condensed than the newer editions. Their format resembles a festival or a conference that focuses on lectures, public programs, and international guests for a local audience, rather than on appealing exhibitions.

Last year, in North America, the Chicago Architecture Biennial celebrated its second and constituting edition. The biennial focused on several foundational modern and postmodern moments and participants were commissioned to make an appeal to those histories. In South America, the Architecture and Urbanism Biennale Chile honored its 20th anniversary with an activist stance. In Europe, the Vienna Biennale on Art, Architecture, and Design also held its second edition and, in Asia, the Seoul Architecture and Urbanism Biennale was launched. The latter two problematized post-humanism: the first intended to restate contemporary values by defining a digital humanism focusing primarily on robotics and bio-technology; the second, however, defined humans in a wider network of things embedded in the commons exploring the relation between design and cosmopolitics.

A great deal of criticism—sometimes simplified but necessary—has been dedicated to the frequently slanted lists of participants regarding their capability to equally represent global interests and tendencies. More than 75% of the participants in Chile were Latin Americans (53% were Chileans), more than 60% in Vienna were Europeans (18% were Austrian), more than 50% in Seoul were Asian (11% were Korean). Local presence varies, but the statistics show the importance of the region over the nation. Chile explored the potential of the regional connection as one of its aims was to explicitly reinforce the relation between Global South practices and professionals. U.S. American participation in Chicago was high (36%) but European offices were actually a majority.

PRESENTNESS

As a platform for architectural thought that is lively and different, biennials usually cost less, may reach a wider public, and bring together more diverse practices and opinions than a building or a publication. For attendees, the draw of the biennial is to be present to debate (or chat)—preferably during the opening days. Standing questions might be answered, and new ones, which promise to be answered in the following event, are sure to be triggered. New biennials and editions are already filling next year's calendar, creating a continuous schedule all around the globe. With culture's financing capital being spent on exhibition formats and plane tickets, is Koolhaas's paradigmatic *archaeologue* actually a curator?[4]

Funding a biennial is cheaper and has a more immediate impact for a city than a star-architect building. Municipal administrations increasingly incorporate such events in their annual budget as a city branding strategy. Instead of being financed by cultural institutions, foundations, or private developers, they are mostly supported by the local authority, using an innovative way of promotion that profits from the so-called 'creative economy' and stimulates a culturally-oriented tourist industry. Most cities give strong arguments for why their biennial has to happen in exactly that location as they rely

on history to create a curatorial narrative. Press releases highlight the architectural significance of the host city: the Chicago Architecture Biennial drew upon Chicago's skyscraping tradition (a reputation that was itself cemented in the 1922 competition), the Seoul Architecture and Urbanism Biennale accentuated Seoul's logistical competence, and the Vienna Biennale revived its modern, avant-gardist spirit from the end of the 18th century.

Biennials are not about the exhibited objects but the experience as a whole. In that sense, architecture has an immense advantage over art: as Aaron Betsky has put it, "architecture is the only art that represents and presents at the same time."[5] There are two basic curating strategies: either designing frameworks or working selectively on the things to be included in the exhibition. For instance, in Chicago, the Artistic Directors' concept was inspired by the impressions of the *Strada Novissima* at the first *Biennale Architettura di Venezia* of 1980, which was conceived as an immersive space. Being an 'administrator of space,' the architect as a curator has the expertise to engage with the first strategy, to blur the spatial limit between exhibit and architecture, and to squeeze the potential of the framework in order to enhance the sensorial, esthetic, and political experience while exploring modes of self-representation. As Pedro Gadanho states, "curating became an author-based practice rather than a merely organizational one, and with this subtle alteration comes also the possibility for other, more subjective critical projects."[6]

COLLECTIVENESS

The biennial is becoming a collective experiment: first it is a group effort and later a group show. Building and caring for a team is primordial. One connected group of locals and internationals comprised of architects, artists, photographers, cultural theorists, scientists, whoever, can be organized according to themes, status,

regions, categories, actuality. Grouping in national pavilions has become outdated as specially commissioned entries are more flexible to enter the curatorial narratives. Nowadays, there is a mix of commissioned, selected, and competed works that ensure the heterogeneity of the group. Exhibitions at the Architecture and Urbanism Biennale Seoul responded, on the one hand, to specific thematic sections, and in fifty city projects, on the other. Chile, for example, held two open calls: to choose the curatorial team and to select contributors along the invited participants.

The public is a different collective. Expanding on Grima's statement, the biennial as a laboratory could involve the public to test architecture and vice versa. In the statement for the upcoming *Biennale Architettura di Venezia*, curators Yvonne Farrell and Shelley McNamara state that "With the theme of 'Freespace,' the *Biennale Architettura* 2018 will present for public scrutiny examples, proposals, elements—built or unbuilt—of work that exemplifies essential qualities of architecture." Are curators responsible for making architecture understandable and interesting for non-architects, for 'public-scrutiny'? As biennials intend to open disciplinary debates to a bigger audience, the public remains an unexplored group. How to reach them is one key question that is only incidentally addressed by the commitment of the architect-curator-designer to the whole spatial experience. The conveyance between architecture, culture, and the public, presents a challenge for evidencing a 'freespace,' a hiatus, still awaiting further reflection.

4   Rem Koolhaas famously stated that "The archaeologue (= archaeology with more interpretation) of the 20th century needs unlimited plane tickets, not a shovel." Rem Koolhaas, "The Generic City". New York: The Monacelli Press, Inc., 1995.

5   Aaron Betsky in conversation with Javier Agustín Rojas. In: "Plot", n. 34, December 2016.

6   Pedro Gadanho, "Is Curating the New Criticism?" In: "Architecture Beyond Criticism: Expert Judgement and Performance Evaluation". New York: Routledge, 2015.

MAKE NEW HISTORY
II Chicago Architecture Biennial

DATE: September 16, 2017 – January 7, 2018 / LOCATION: Chicago, Illinois, USA / ARTISTIC CO-DIRECTORS: Mark Lee and Sharon Johnston / EXECUTIVE DIRECTOR: Todd Palmer / MAIN VENUE: Chicago Cultural Center / WEB: chicagoarchitecturebiennial.org

"Make New History," the much discussed second Chicago Architecture Biennial, showcased the work of slightly more participants than its first edition. It rested on Chicago's rich architectural and modern heritage to consolidate a venue that optimistically discussed the discipline's future. Since mid-September and until the beginning of 2018, Chicago's Cultural Center and other locations across town, such as community-based museums, hosted architecture exhibitions, and related events.

The City of Chicago and the Biennial Committee, co-organizers of the event, announced that the Artistic Co-Directors would be Sharon Johnston and Mark Lee (founding partners at Johnston Marklee and Associates) in September 2016. They chose the title, inspired by a provocative Ed Ruscha piece. "Make New History," published in 2009, is a book of six hundred empty white pages; the Artistic Directors were eager to fill them. In the catalogue, Sarah Herda (Co-Artistic Director of the first biennial) describes their work as a "collecting activity" that gathers "building histories, material histories, image histories, and civic histories;" in other words, a collection of references and architectural events re-enacted.

The selected participants were specifically commissioned to produce new work that reflected on stories of the last one hundred years of western architectural thought, with the aim of constructing a possible present and future in a strict exhibition format. Intended to engage a wider public, the biennial uses easily understandable titles, large scale models, and performative spaces. After four months of construction, Chicago's Cultural Center transformed into an immersive environment that became a playful landscape for a non-expert audience.

One of the main exhibitions, the "Vertical City," was based on Stanley Tigerman's 1980 "Late Entries" exhibit, which, was in turn

Installation view of Horizontal City at G.A.R Hall, 2017, Courtesy of Chicago Architecture Biennial, Kendall McCaugherty © Hall Merrick Photographers

Installation view of Vertical City at Sidney R. Yates Hall, 2017, Courtesy of Chicago Architecture Biennial, Steve Hall © Hall Merrick Photographers

inspired by the 1922 Chicago Tribune Tower Competition. 16 towers, which respect the height and perimeter of the original competition, emerged in a four by four grid in Yates Hall. The second main exhibition, the "Horizontal City," turns GAR Hall into the "Room of Plinths" which recovers the plan of the 1947 Illinois Institute by Mies van der Rohe. In this case, 24 practices converted a historically-relevant interior photograph of their choice into a model that speculated on both representational techniques and its actuality. Also on view at the Cultural Center was "A Love of the World," a show curated by Jesus Vassallo on photography, architecture, and the built environment.[7]

A section of special projects included: a collaboration between SO – IL and Ana Prvački, a François Perrin installation at the Garfield Park Conservatory, and a Gerard & Kelly performance at the Farnsworth House, among others. A comprehensible list of free public programs, including lectures, forums, discussions, and films, completed the list of activities. The lecture series "Now + Then: Occasional History" was a restaging of the 1982 Charlottesville Tapes.

In the aftermath, critics were concerned with both curatorial and discursive strategies. Matt Shaw (Arch Paper), suggested that "the complexity of history was re-

7   NESS invited Stan Allen and Jesus Vassallo to converse around this and other topics in THE DOSSIER (see p. 98).

duced to precedent." In a similar register, Léa-Catherine Szacka (Domus) suggested that the contemporary context is quite different from that of 1980 and asked: "Faced with a theoretical and ideological vacuum, against whom and what can young architects take a stance?" Phillip Denny (Volume) noticed the excluded, rather than the exhibited; "It should not be read as a map of the field in this moment, but perhaps more like a tendentious complement to everything it leaves out of the picture, something more akin to a portrait." Mimi Zeiger (Dezeen) noted a curatorial narrowness, which converted the act of viewing into a comparative act. Given this scenario, what is the history being discussed? Can the paradigmatic use of the after image literally become the ground for a productive discussion, or will it represent a nostalgic parenthesis in the history of architecture?

ROBOTS. WORK. OUR FUTURE
II Biennale for Art, Design, and Architecture Vienna

DATE: June 21, 2017 – October 1, 2017 / LOCATION: Vienna, Austria / DIRECTOR: Christoph Thun-Hohenstein / CURATORIAL TEAM: Anne Faucheret, Angelika Fitz, Anab Jain, Amelie Klein, Elke Krasny, Marlies Wirth, Harald Gruendl, Ulrike Haele and Martina Fineder / MAIN VENUE: Austrian Museum of Applied Arts and Contemporary Art / WEB: viennabiennale.org

The Vienna Biennale 2017 is an initiative of the Austrian Museum of Applied Arts and Contemporary Art (MAK) organized conjunctly with the University of Applied Arts Vienna, the Kunsthalle Wien, the Architekturzentrum Wien (AZW), the Vienna Business Agency, and the Austrian Institute of Technology. Lasting the extent of the European summer, the event combined art, design, and architecture in a city that treasures its tradition as a site of the modern avant-garde.

Christoph Thun-Hohenstein, the General Director of the MAK, was Executive and Creative Director of the biennial. The curators, professionals experienced in curating architecture and art, faithfully represented the organizing institutions. The team included Anne Faucheret (Curator at the Kunsthalle Wien), Angelika Fitz (Curator and Director at the Architek-

turzentrum Wien), Anab Jain (Co-founder and Director at Superflux in London and Professor at the University of Applied Arts Vienna), Amelie Klein (Curator at the Vitra Design Museum in Weil am Rhein), Elke Krasny (Independent Curator and Professor of Art and Education at the Academy of Fine Arts Vienna), Marlies Wirth (Curator in Digital Culture and Design Collection at the MAK), and lastly, representing the Institute of Design Research Vienna, Harald Gruendl, Ulrike Haele and Martina Fineder).

"Robots. Work. Our Future" proposed a seemingly impossible—or at least contradictory—task: to look for the human in the post-human. The biennial embraced a "Digital Humanism" in order to transmit a message of optimism, an alternative orientation to people in which, "creative ideas and artistic projects [...] help improve the world," says the press release. According to Thun-Hohenstein, "work is central to our prosperity and our well-being. Automation and robotics break down barriers, especially between humans and machines. Addressing and helping to humanely shape these elementary changes

triggered by digital modernity is a key aim of the Vienna Biennale 2017."

Robots, hybrids, and uncanny businesses, entered the discussions in the commons, as well as shared economies and the maker's movement. The biennial was organized into three exhibitions. The first, "Hello Robot: Design between Human and Machine," was displayed in different parts of Vienna and primarily dealt with the exploration of the robotic in the everyday. Artists, including Alfredo Jaar, architectural forerunners Friedrich Kiesler, Archigram, and Greg Lynn, music icons Björk and Kraftwerk, film-maker Spike Jonze, among others, all shared the stage. The second exhibit, "How Will We Work?" explored speculations on automation and industry in works by Harun Farocki, automato.farm, Sam Lavigne, and others. The last exhibit, "CityFactory: New Work. New Design," took over different spaces across the city that problematized work in regards to creation, society, and sustainability, with displays by Jesko Fezer, Andres Jaque, and Refugee Nation, to name a few. Public programs included "Care + Repair," situated as a critical workspace; "Work it, feel it!" which

Exhibition View "ARTIFICIAL TEARS. Singularity & Humanness—A Speculation," MAK Exhibition Hall
© Aslan Kudrnofsky/MAK

completed the discussion reflecting on the fleshy body in the digital age; "Artificial Tears: Singularity & Humanness—A Speculation" travelled to dystopian futures; and, "I don't know" rehearsed innovative, growing relations between things.

As inaugurated at the 3ʳᵈ Istanbul Design Biennale, the Vienna Biennale 2017 cooperated with E-flux Architecture to launch a series of articles and critical essays under the title, "Artificial Labor," which can be accessed online.The catalog also extends the event's circulation with contributions by Pedro Gadanho and Maria Lind, among others.

Installation View of Hashim Sarkis, "Byblos Blue,"
Courtesy of Architecture and Urbanism Biennale Chile.
Ph. Pablo Blanco Barros

DIÁLOGOS IMPOSTERGABLES
XX Bienal de Arquitectura y Urbanismo Chile

DATE: October 26, 2017 – November 10, 2017 / LOCATION: Valparaíso, Chile / EXECUTIVE DIRECTOR AND GENERAL CURATOR: Felipe Vera / CREATIVE DIRECTOR AND CURATOR OF SPECIAL PROJECTS: Rodrigo Tisi / CURATORIAL TEAM: Miguel Cancino, Claudio Magrini, José Mayoral, Pola Mora, Pablo Navarrete, and Jeannette Sordi / MAIN VENUE: Parque Cultural de Valparaíso / WEB: impostergable.cl/en

The Architecture and Urbanism Biennial Chile recently celebrated its twentieth anniversary. It was organized by the *Colegio de Arquitectos de Chile* in collaboration with the Association of the Offices of Architecture and the Network of Architecture Schools. The organizers described the anniversary edition as having a double objective: it would bring the discussion on architecture and the city closer to society and position the event internationally.

The *Colegio de Arquitectos de Chile* held a public call to select the event's curators. The competition was won by a team of Chilean and international architects as well as specialists from other disciplines. The Executive Director and General Curator was Felipe Vera, who was accompanied by the Creative Director and Curator of Special Projects, Rodrigo Tisi. Jeannette Sordi and José Mayoral worked as curators of the Academy section and Pola Mora served as the curator of the Professionals section. Miguel Cancino and Claudio Magrini were curators of Activism and Territorial Contributions, and, finally, Pablo Navarrete was curator of the Public Sec-

tor. In a second open call, the committee selected 58 contributions from a pool of more than four hundred applicants, to participate alongside invited guests.

With the title "Diálogos impostergables" ("Unpostponable Dialogues"), the event ambitioned to "establish a South to South dialogue, reimagining the relationship between the generative forces of cities and effectively including those that reside in the margins." The acknowledgement of a Global South prepared the ground to discuss shared problems and opportunities while, at the same time, assuming the active role local players take in the shaping of the environment, without the mediation of external representation.

What is architecture's agency? How can its practitioners make the most out of the tools they have on hand? The biennial was an invitation to reflect and dialogue, and was organized into seven sections: Identity, Commons, Participation, Integration, Vulnerability, Resources, and Future. Various formats of conversations took place on the central stage: public discussions, verbal wrestling, and inspirational talks about empowerment, collaboration, and coexistence, among others. According to Felipe Vera's opening remarks in the catalogue, the 'unpostponable' sets the priorities of a public agenda in a biennial that is "not only commemorative but also provocative, a stimulation to take action."

A series of photographed portraits of migrants and Chileans by Jorge Brantmayer hung throughout the main venue and unified

the biennial's narrative. The focus was put on people and the connections they establish with the built environment and shared resources, rather than architectural projects. Unlike other biennials, a high proportion of representatives from the public sector from Chile, Colombia, Brazil, and Argentina, and in particular a number of activists, shared the stage with the usual audience. Following the line of the *Biennale Architettura di Venezia*, curated by fellow Chilean Alejandro Aravena, the aim was to design a conversation and to assume dialogue as a mode of practice that could exceed the discipline's borders and engage critically, discursively, provocatively but, nevertheless, responsively.

Curators Felipe Vera and José Mayoral co-edited with Lots of Architecture Publishers the first issue of a monographic series dedicated to the work and thoughts of Hashim Sarkis Studios. –NESS.docs 1 features seven projects, essays, and conversations between Angelo Bucci, Stan Allen, Kenneth Frampton, and Sarkis. His installation "Byblos Blue," a committed study on the historical center of the city of Byblos in Lebanon, was on view at the Architecture and Urbanism Biennial Chile in the "Special Projects" section. Given this opportunity, –NESS.docs 1 was officially presented by the NESS editorial team together with Felipe Vera, Jose Mayoral, and Hashim Sarkis, along with Rodrigo Perez de Arce, Adjunct Professor at the Catholic University Chile).

Installation View at the Dongdaemun Design Plaza.
Courtesy of Biennale of Architecture and Urbanism Seoul.
© urbannext.com

IMMINENT COMMONS
I Biennale of Architecture and Urbanism Seoul

DATE: September 1, 2017 – November 5, 2017 / LOCATION: Seoul, South Korea / CO-DIRECTORS: Hyungmin Pai and Alejandro Zaera Polo / CURATORIAL TEAM: Youngseok Lee, Jeffrey S. Anderson, Helen Hejung Choi, Yerin Kang, Jie-Eun Hwang, Hyewon Lee, Soo-in Yang, and Kyung Jae Kim / MAIN VENUE: Dongdaemun Design Plaza / WEB: seoulbiennale.org

The Biennale of Architecture and Urbanism Seoul is the result of a rather intense municipal labor. Over the past several years, the metropolitan government has created the Urban Space Improvement Bureau and the position of the Seoul City Architect, who is responsible for the Seoul Design Foundation and consequently for the organization of the biennial. According to Clare Lyster, Seoul is "the Paradigmatic Logistical City," a perfect location for the committed and productive of the contemporary, global city.[8]

When Hyungmin Pai and Alejandro Zaera Polo were appointed to co-direct the biennial, they asked: "Does the scenario, determined by the rise of the Anthropocene and the crisis of neo-liberal capitalism, imply that the work of urbanists and ar-

chitects has become futile? Has urbanism been expelled from politics, now at the mercy of capital redistribution?"[9] The curators explained that the event was conceived as "an experimental platform for an imminent urbanism that goes beyond human-centered function, ownership, and consumption to a common of resources, technologies, and production." The biennial asked some pressing questions, constructing a dialectical relation between technological advancement, on the one hand, and its ecological, social, political, and ethical implications, on the other.

The main thematic exhibition was "Nine Commons" curated by Youngseok Lee and Jeffrey S. Anderson. In their pursuit to imagine a 'post-human cosmology,' they proposed revisiting the four ecological commons, Air, Water, Fire, and Earth, and the five technological commons, Making, Moving, Communicating, Sensing, and Recycling. This meant that issues of jurisdiction over ubiquitous commons, hydrologic initiatives, biotechnologies, food

production, management of waste, urban transport infrastructures, domestic control mechanisms, flows of information and privacy, among other hybrid territories and polemical, complex issues, were discussed.

Inversely, the cities exhibition turned to local experiences. "Commoning Cities" was curated by Helen Hejung Choi with the assistance of Hyoeun Kim and Donghwa Kang. It presented a selection of public initiatives, projects, narratives of rapid urbanization, and cases of scarcity and privatization. The exhibit gathered more than 40 experiences from around the globe. Additional activities and public programs included international studios, film and video screenings, workshops, lectures, and guided tours. The biennial focused on the problem of food production in the "Urban Foodshed," curated by Hyewon Lee, and on mobility in, "Walking the Commons," curated by Soo-in Yang and Kyung Jae Kim. In partnership with Municipal Projects Seoul, the programs at the biennial ambitioned to intervene in the

8   Clare Lyster. "Seoul: Genealogy of a Logistical Ecosystem." In: Alejandro Zaera Polo and Jeffrey S. Anderson (ed.). "Imminent Commons: The Expanded City." Actar Publishers and Seoul Biennale of Architecture and Urbanism, 2017.

9   The 'Anthropocene' is a scientific term that designates the impact of human behavior on the earth's surface, ecosystem, and atmosphere as the defining trait of our contemporary geological era.

actual fabric of the city and to turn theoretical discussion into contextualized and consistent measures.

A collaboration with the digital platform urbanNext and the production of three catalogues that include curatorial texts by the directors and contributions by the participants, as well as essays by Saskia Sassen, Charles Waldheim, Beatriz Colomina, and Mario Carpo, furthered discussion of the contents of the biennial. The catalogues, conceived as 'knowledge making *dispositifs*,' extend beyond the temporal frame of the initial event and try to subvert the ephemerality inherent in the biennial phenomenon with written evidence, to be used as openers for future theoretical debates.

INCONCLUSIVENESS

Once the event has finished, what is left—apart from the hangover from opening night—is the catalogue, a photographic and digital archive. Only rarely are exhibits purchased by a museum for its collections; sometimes a thinned version of the exhibition travels to other locations. Biennials have the characteristic of being open-ended, their conclusions are slippery and difficult to grasp. For instance, in Chile, the last paragraph of the catalogue's introduction reads: "It will not end with its closing date but will transcend through propositions, projects, and actions that arise from it." Therefore, it is hard to say that the biennial is a refuge, because things do not end up taking a precise form or formulating a concise message. Or, does its comfort actually reside in the inconclusiveness? Some curatorial statements can be provocative or trendy but, as a publicly funded event, the risks for them to become institutionalized and lose their experimental ground are high. Yet, it is encouraging to look at spaces in which architecture can be discussed in a festive, extravagant way. While waiting for the biennials on the 2018 calendar, fingers are crossed for a critical re-enactment of the *Deutscher Werkbund* Exposition of 1927.

Seoul. Courtesy of Biennale of Architecture and Urbanism Seoul,
© urbannext.com

IMMINENT COMMONS
CATALOGUE SERIES
Published by Actar Publishers, and the Seoul Biennale of Architecture and Urbanism 2017.

URBAN QUESTIONS FOR THE NEAR FUTURE
Edited by Alejandro Zaera-Polo, Hyungmin Pai, and urbanNext

"The first publication of the Seoul Biennale of Architecture and Urbanism 2017, proposes a framework where set basic commons—an evolving network of agencies, resources and technologies—are the critical issue in the move towards a sustainable and just urbanism. It shows an exploration not of distant utopias, but of the very near future."

THE EXPANDED CITY
Edited by Alejandro Zaera-Polo and Jeffrey S. Anderson

"The second book presents contemporary urbanism thoughts on nine imminent commons, which engage collective ecological and technological resources relevant to all cities and even extra-urban territories."

COMMONING CITIES
Edited by Hyungmin Pai and Helen Hejung Choi

"Commoning Cities presents questions and answers concerning the current state and near future of cities of the world through the lens of public initiatives, projects, and urban narratives."

SO–IL

1

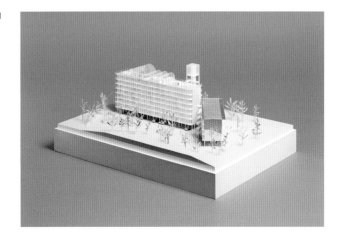

2

As they explore the fields of architecture, urban planning, landscape, research, and teaching, these French architects focus on their own list of essentials: designing is for them an experience between strategy and form, rigor and freedom, the specific and the generic, the immediate and the progressive. Far from any dogma, they seek a synthetic formal clarity that could provide a building with a wide malleability of uses. They intend to produce a kind of architecture free from mannerisms, typologies, or trends.

5

4

1 – Site's reconversion, Mérignac, France, 2013-2017.   2 – Housing Competition on Chapelle International masterplan for the "LOT F", Paris, France, 2014.   3 – Bruther's office.
4 – Offices, Rehabilitation and Expansion of a High Rise Building, Paris, France, 2015.   5 – Texture Samples.   6 – Guggenheim Helsinki Design Competition, Finland, 2014.
7 – Learning Center, Brussels, Belgium, 2016.   /   Photos: Julien Hourcade.   /   Portrait Photos: José Gallego.

Alexandre Theriot

3

Bruther

6

Stéphanie Bru

7

About Spaces and Freedom of Choice

Bruther interviewed by Javier Agustín Rojas

Throughout several encounters, this conversation assembles fragments of lectures, conferences, and other informal exchanges. In over ten years of practice, Bruther has mainly worked with public commissions, actively participating in international open competitions.

JAVIER AGUSTÍN ROJAS

As Philip Ursprung mentions in his recent essay about your work, Liberty and Beauty: Bruther's Architecture and the Reach of Play: "The list of built and non-built projects [of Bruther] reads like an inventory of the welfare-state typology: New Generation Research Center, Residence for Researchers, Cultural and Sports Center, Central Library, Housing Units and Shops, Housing Units, Day-care Center and Kindergarten, School Group, Boarding School, Gymnasium and Cultural Center, Housing Units, Social Residence and Cultural Center, Day- care Center, Convent and Chapel, Visual Arts Museum."[1] Did you have a specific aim to address these programs when you both founded the office? How do you choose which competitions to take part in?

ALEXANDRE THERIOT

For us, architecture is a place to share and spend time with other people. We believe we have a responsibility as architects to work in that direction, especially nowadays, so we've always tried to apply to competitions related to the public realm. In that sense, for us there are two types of competitions. First there are the ones in France, where you have publications to check different announcements and decide whether to apply or not. In this sense, the French system is easy, and the only hard thing is to get selected when you are just starting out. The other type of competitions we participate in are the international and open. In those cases, our approach is different. We use them as a way to build references—because when you start your own office, obviously, you don't have any—which could later help us get selected in our own country.

JAR   Did you deliberately decide not to take part in private competitions?

AT   We did a lot of competitions for private investors when we started out. We used those experiences to start building a catalogue and to apply to new ones. The first competition we were selected for was for a kindergarten for Paris's City Hall. In the end, we did not win, but people started to know about us and our approach. We did a lot more and we lost a lot more, but step by step we managed to get selected for some, especially in Paris—where we live and work—and in the north of France, in Lille.

JAR   When did you finish your first built project?

AT   In 2013. It took us five years to finish our first building, which was fifty Housing Units at Limeil-Brévannes. All of the offices that started to work at the same time as we did build a lot before us. During those years, friends used to ask us what were we doing, and we said, "Well, we are trying to win competitions and build them, but it is not so easy!" We were just not so anxious. [laughs]

Grape Leaves III, Kelly Ellsworth, 1973. In Stéphanie Bru and Alexandre Theriot. "Introduction". Paris: R-diffusion, 2014. Ph. Mariam Samur.

JAR   I think that lack of anxiety is characteristic of your work, in general. There is no anxiety to produce new forms and there is no anxiety to make a statement. Your book,[2] which is made up of only images and drawings, all in the same format, presents a lot of different things but in a very neutral way.

AT   Looking back, I think it was good that we did not build the first project we designed, because we probably were not so good. You need time to build your own preoccupations and to forget what you have learned before working for other offices. But I understand what you mean with anxiety—we never had any interest in being different, or original, or new.

JAR   You can also learn that by browsing the book. Your references—whether they are works of art from renowned artists like Ellsworth Kelly, or personal photographs that you like—are shown at the same level as the competitions, projects, constructive drawings, photographs of built works, and furniture you have made.

AT   That is our attitude, everything is important for us. Sometimes it can be a problem!

JAR   I felt that attitude during the week you spent in Buenos Aires.[3] When we visited a building by adamo-faiden,[4] you paid careful attention to details, such as where the concrete

columns were hidden in the walls behind the white plaster.

AT   Nowadays the conditions of architecture are changing and it is not possible for us to do everything, so that is why we enjoyed adamo-faiden's work so much, because we like that the very small things can be very important.

JAR   To start discussing your work specifically, I would like to ask you about how you deal with form. One can easily trace back your approach towards freedom of use as the main goal of architecture to the work of Lacaton & Vassal, but the overall result in your projects is always more free and imaginative.

AT   That is something we talked about a lot with Jan de Vylder for our monograph in 2G.[5] We took a day to go see our buildings with him and he was obsessed with why we took certain decisions, and that is where the title of his article comes from. Aside from this, you could say that the starting point for the forms we create is always the urban context. We spend a lot of time just finding the right way to manage the installation of a project on a certain site. That is also why we included a lot of pictures about the context of our buildings in our book.

JAR   It is as if your architecture has a monumentality or a certain presence that is not derived from its program or its meaning but by its form, or even by its objectuality.

AT   We do not care about form by itself but we believe in the capacity of form to organize an urban space and create a certain dynamic. For instance, in Kelly Ellsworth's drawings, you can see something similar: you have a line, then you have a curve and another line, and incidentally there is a space between them with certain characteristics. We experiment a lot during the development of a project, and we try to understand what a certain curve or a small change of angle can provoke in a space. But we cannot explain why something is a triangle and not a square, or the other way around. That is why we also give so much importance to technique, because it is the only way to justify a project and it ends this type of conversation about sensibilities. Architecture is the act of building, so it is rational, it is linked with technical qualities and with gravity, and so on, but we also believe it is a feeling towards a certain situation or topic.

JAR   You can see this, for example, in the slightly curved façades of the Cultural and Sports Center in Saint-Blaise, which gives the building a much more sensual appearance, as opposed to if it were a simple box. The detail is very simple, you have only changed the position of each glass, but there are no custom curved pieces of any kind. What was the design methodology for this project?

HELSINKI
CENTRAL LIBRARY
Cultural Complex, international competition entry

Ph. Julien Hourcade

AT When we received the brief, the client wanted a very small and low project because they thought it was the best solution in order not to create any conflict or distress in the area. Step by step, after analyzing the situation and developing several ideas, we understood this was not the right attitude for this urban context, and we decided to do a really compact and vertical building. By breaking the client's imperative, the dimension and the relationship of the project with the landscape was now different.

All the work we do is commanded by this same attitude. We try to find the right question for each competition. The client has its own, but you also have to find something that you believe in for each project. So, the first part of the process is always the same—we do not know which way to go, and we try to keep this freshness or innocence towards the program and the site for a while. We develop several ideas—for a competition we can do about twenty—playing with the requirements of the program or seeking a certain archetypical typology before deciding which project is the best proposal. That is the most difficult moment for us, because you have to make a decision and you are never sure which way to go! We also like it a lot: it is full of stress, the time is very short, and you have to be very focused on the project, because if you win it this will define what you will develop, draw, and build over the next years.

JAR What tools do you work with when doing a project now?

AT We work a lot with plans, we draw many of them. You could say the plan is the main element of our work—it is where the essence of each project lies. We do not draw as many section, that comes as a result of the urban context, of regulations such as setbacks and so on, and we conceive it more as a technical element than the plan. We only work with 3D software in the end, when you have to produce a specific image that is the result of all the thinking you developed during the design process.

JAR You also produce very beautiful models for all of your projects. Does this happen at the end as well?

AT No, we work with models during the process. We need them as an abstract tool to make choices. When you do a perspective or an image with the computer it is much harder to change your mind about a project. To make a decision, we do not think about whether something looks nice or not. We try to focus on more abstract things like dimensions, volumes, and forms. Again, decisions are difficult, so for us it is important to use tools that help us take them correctly. That is why representation—plans, drawings, models—is so important. And the rest of the choices that come later, like what the façade looks like, will be more linked to technical questions than to composition.

JAR It is true that in all the office's projects the façade looks

MARILYN LIT

Marilyn lit.
Autour d'elle, une jungle paisible dans laquelle
poussent les idées. On y trouve des arbres
de ténacité, des fleurs de doute, des baies
d'énergie, des fruits de débat et des plantes à
sarcasmes. On y cultive des états d'âme et l'art
de l'attitude. On peut s'extraire du monde tout
en le contemplant. On y permet la convergence,
on y crée la connexion entre les disciplines, on y
décuple les connaissances, on y imagine la foule,
on y est citoyen, on y est accueilli, on y grandit,
on s'y accomplit, on s'y sent libre, on y paresse,
on y dort. C'est une bulle posée sur un dehors
trop vaste. C'est le royaume des passeurs de
savoirs. C'est une forêt dans laquelle il ne pleut
jamais. Et le temps qui passe n'y changera rien.

more like an ensemble of different elements than a composition larger than itself?

AT   For us, façades are technical filters made of several layers, each one with a specific function. With glass, you can manage light and views, and most of the time we like to do very transparent façades to bring the landscape into the building. If you have a really large glass façade, then your room is no longer just limited by four walls—it's larger than itself and more related to the surrounding landscape. Sometimes we work with translucent surfaces just to get the light but not the views, and also with curtains that change the relationship between the inside and the outside. You can also work with different elements on the outside, like *brise soleil* to control the sun impact. And, of course, if you need fresh air then you put a window. So, our façades are made of all of these different elements and we try to play with them.

JAR   In your projects, structure also looks very playful and agile, like the V-shaped columns in Saint-Blaise [p. 138] or the massive open plan in the New Generation Research Center [p. 148] created by the steel beams.

AT   The story is different from project to project. In those that you mentioned, the decisions were made at different moments. For Saint-Blaise, we realized very quickly that we had to work with a square plan with columns in the corners, but the distance on each side was too long. So instead of adding a new column or having really thick beams, we developed this beam-column or V-shaped column which gives the project more lightness.
In Caen, the fundamental decision was to work with an open plan and have all the fixed functions on the outside. The decision to make the slabs in steel and the columns in concrete was taken later for more simple and economic reasons.

JAR   In several of Bruther's projects, one can easily find references to architectural history. Some may seem obvious, like the galvanized exterior staircases of the Science de la Vie Building at EPFL [p. 170] that you designed with BAUKUNST, which resembles Lloyd's building by Richard Rogers (1986). There are other more silent quotes, like the structural design of the New Generation Research Center, which reminds us of the structural extravaganza of Claude Parent's Maison de l'Iran (Paris,1960-1968). What is your interest in history and how does it relate to your design process?

AT   Our mind is full of images, historical or not, and to be honest, sometimes there is no relationship between all of them. It is like an imaginary field, and we believe we are part of a really long chain of elements that can be

BERLIN MUSEUM FOR THE 20TH CENTURY

Contemporary Art Museum, international competition entry

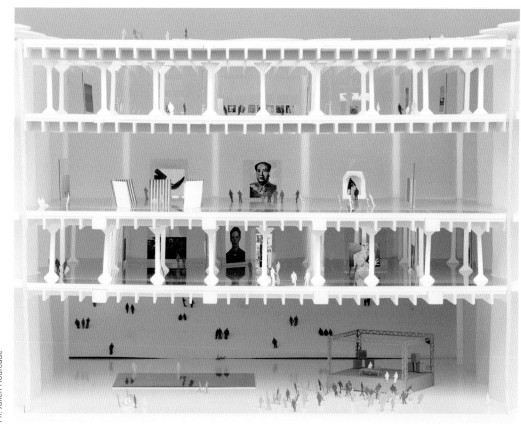

Ph. Julien Hourcade

connected or approached. So, it's really easy to catch these references and that is not a problem for us. We like Richard Rogers's and Louis Kahn's architecture, for example, because of the relationship between the different elements and the obvious organizational aspects of their work. You can almost read a story in every plan, and understand why suddenly something is twisted or not. I mean, for us the plan is not just the result of a technical problem but more like an ecosystem in which every element has its own identity and relationship with the others. We believe the whole project can be understood as a certain juxtaposition of things—you can have an attitude towards the urban context, another one for the program, and a different one for the materials—and everything you develop later for each of these elements is independent of the rest. There is no hierarchy in the final result. We do not think subordination in architecture is necessary. The connections between the different elements can be loose.

JAR   Does this also have to do with your idea of *bricolage*?[5]

AT   Yes, exactly. Nowadays many architects try to develop new things constantly: new typologies, new forms, new materials. For us, it is different: we do not care so much about inventing. We interpret, we assemble, we put things together in order to create new situations, and that is all. There is no vindictive attitude in this—it is just about the

feeling that you can put two different things together and the results can be interesting. Of course, it is not something that happens easily or randomly.

JAR   To finish our conversation, I would like you to talk about what Bruther's architecture seeks to do, in the end. You have stated in a brief text in your book: "It is not so much beauty we are after, but liberty." What does liberty mean for you?

AT   The first idea of freedom we have is about our attitude—what we try to keep in mind in our daily life—and it has to do with staying as open-minded as possible, whatever the context. It is the freedom to take a decision because you feel it is the right way but you cannot explain why. It is to assume that we work with feelings and sensibilities because we are human beings. Right now, it is quite difficult to say "I believe in this or that" so we like to think more of it as a state of mind.

In terms of architecture, we conceive freedom as a way of not fixing things in time. That is why the organization of a plan is so important. We try to keep spaces open, or think that a building could be used differently than we imagined. Freedom means that architecture is not an absolute. It has an unfinished dimension, and the process does not end when you finish a building. Freedom means that architecture is not absolute. We think that architecture has an unfinished dimension, and that the process doesn't end when you finish a building. Maybe it is better to keep a certain

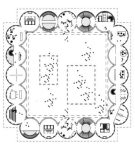

MISCELLANÉES

L'usine à produire de l'imaginaire tournait à plein régime. Dans le parcours en enfilade, on pouvait voir toutes sortes de gens faire toutes sortes de choses. Un jeune homme promenait son regard sur l'échine brisée du temps. Le progrès et la catastrophe ponctuaient l'espace. L'exposition défilait sous les yeux émerveillés des visiteurs. Un couple assis sur un banc observait Berlin changer tour à tour de masque. En fond sonore se jouait la symphonie d'une grande ville. La foule constituait un héros aux mille visages. Une femme tentait de distinguer l'hybride du morcelé fondus en un bloc. Les piliers de béton soutenaient un ciel doux. Les silos accumulés ne formaient plus qu'une grande machine. Une fois son mouvement enclenché, il se passait inévitablement quelque chose. Ces fragments de vie étaient autant de manières de construire des mondes.

distance and respect the way people want to use it.

JAR You have worked on this topic with different collaborators, such as video makers, On Architecture (Felipe De Ferrari and Diego Grass) or photographers, Maxime Delvaux and Julien Hourcade. As I have written before,[6] I think these precise visual documentations are not silent celebrations of appropriation, but documents that allow us (and the architects themselves) to really understand the nature of the buildings. Many times, the images do not document the objects themselves but some new points in space they allow, and their subsequent views towards the periphery. In others, they portray rather surreal uses—as in one video of Saint-Blaise that shows the little wooden volume of the ground floor full of children playing with parrots.

AT For us, that represents a research field. We are convinced that these documents translate architecture. All of the time you have to explain what you do and what you are trying to do, but sometimes it is quite difficult to do it because you are simply not the best at understanding yourself. I have the feeling—and I am quite sure about this—that it is very difficult to watch yourself in the mirror and to describe what you see exactly. At the same time, it is really important to understand what is actually going on with a building after it is finished. When you draw it, you spend so much time thinking about the people who will use it, that you have to go back later to check how big the gap with reality was. And, of course, there are many gaps … Because life is so much stronger than architecture. For example, every time we go to Caen there is something different. Sometimes you find people dancing in the rooms, or attending a lecture, or building furniture. And that is a really good feedback, because nothing is always perfect, but you are able to see that you took good decisions.

1 Philip Ursprung. "Liberty and Beauty: Bruther's Architecture and the Reach of Play," published in 2G n° 76 Bruther. Berlin: Koenig Books, 2017.
2 Stéphanie Bru and Alexandre Theriot. "Introduction." Paris: Bruther, 2014.
3 adamo-faiden is an Argentinian office founded by Sebastian Adamo and Marcelo Faiden in 2007. adamo-faiden.com
4 Jan de Vylder. "What cannot be understood and what should not be understood." Published in 2G n° 76 Bruther. Berlin: Koenig Books, 2017.
5 Bruther developed this idea in "The reach of the game", a lecture at Monte, Buenos Aires. Available at nessmagazine.com
6 Javier Agustín Rojas. "Never-ending Architecture," published in 2G n° 76 Bruther. Berlin: Koenig Books, 2017.

Saint-Blaise Cultural & Sports Center

The Parisian neighborhood of Saint-Blaise has the highest population density of Europe, but it does not host the diversity of activities, architectures, populations, and uses that one would imagine of such an urban fabric. Situated between two major neighborhood arteries and vectors of activities, the site does not take advantage of this dynamic. The Cultural and Sports Center reacts to this particular situation; it stands as a compact object that releases as much ground space as possible and deploys itself vertically.

Stratified and composite, it displays an architectural vocabulary that takes an opposing stance to its immediate environment. Abstraction rather than the expression of the function, diversity rather than a uniformity of textures and colors, and transparency in the face of the opacity of its surroundings—these are all architectural postures that define the composition of the new Cultural and Sports Center. In the same way, its morphology, subtly curved, grants the project a sculptural character and proposes a rupture with the utilitarian architecture of the surrounding context.

Transparent, the building becomes an 'architecture-link' that establishes new perspectives and connects various facilities within the neighborhood. It participates in a pedestrian space, which livens the area with outdoor activities. Indoors, several degrees of transparency reached by the composing materials spatially organize activities and uses. Generosity is the common denominator of all the proposed spaces. The Saint-Blaise Cultural and Sports Center is a new polarity, a place of convergence, a public space revealed and restored to the public, and an attractive landmark.

The building received the Best Architects 2016 Gold Award Prize and was nominated for the 2015 Mies van der Rohe Prize.

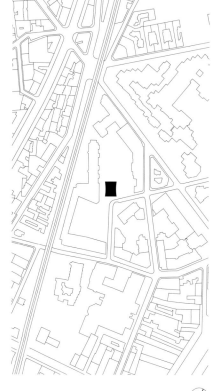

Site Plan

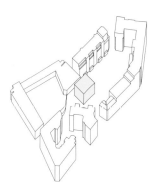

DATE: 2011-2014 / LOCATION: Paris 20th, France / BUILT AREA: 3,000 m² - 31,900 sf / PROGRAM: Sports hall, visual arts halls, music room, offices, and outdoor sports fields / CLIENT: City of Paris / STATUS: Completed, won competition entry / DESIGN TEAM: Bruther / COLLABORATORS: Batiserf, Choulet, Bmf, Altia / PHOTOS: Maxime Delvaux (p. 140, p. 143, p. 144), Filip Dujardin (p. 147), Julien Hourcade (p. 139)

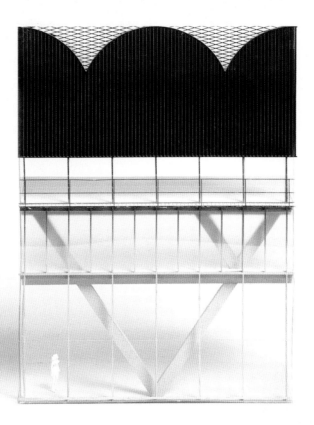

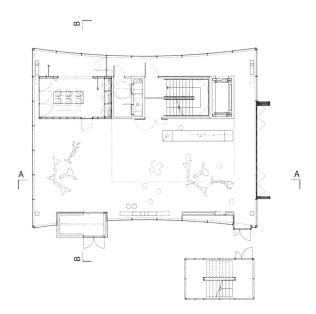

Ground floor

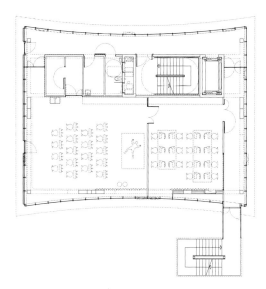

First floor

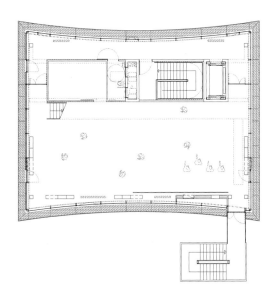

Second floor

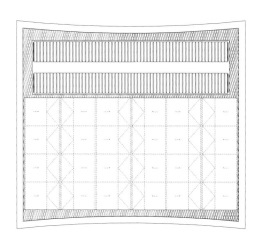

Roof plan

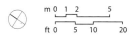

IL Y A

Il y a une enclave.
Il y a un espace public fractionné et opaque parmi les rez-de-chaussée aveugles, il y a des maisons qui ne sont pas la mienne, des maisons qui ne sont pas la vôtre, il y a des maisons qui se ressemblent, il y a les carences d'un quartier dense devenu oppressant, il y a des rues désertées, des espaces dans lesquels on ne fait que passer, des silhouettes peu bavardes, des immeubles de grandes hauteurs aux géométries complexes. Il y a, au loin, un voisin parisien. Il y a, juste là, l'horizon saturé.

Mais il y aussi une arène.
Il y a une muraille qui enclot un grand vide, il y a des interactions potentielles, il y a des espaces piétons, des espaces en devenir, des espaces verts, il y a des murs végétalisés, il y a des équipements scolaires, il y a un écrin bâti, il y a du lien, de la proximité, des logements, un réseau, une vie de quartier qui sommeille. Il y a un monde à révéler.

Il y a un signal.
Il y a un objet ouvert, une machine compacte, un repère qui fédère, un sol qui s'offre au piéton. Il y a un phare qui rayonne tout en ménageant ses distances, il y a une vue dégagée, il y a un paysage dans la ville. Il y a une silhouette singulière aux courbes légères et dimensions réglées, il y a la diversité des textures et la précision des couleurs, il y a une grande transparence, il y a des activités exposées, il y a des lieux d'échange et de convergence, une place couverte résolument publique, il y a un accueil bienveillant. Il y a une urbanité qui anticipe, qui évolue, qui dure. Il y a un univers qui se renouvelle sans cesse.

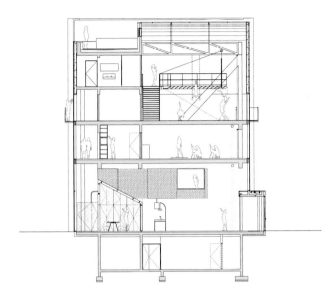

B section

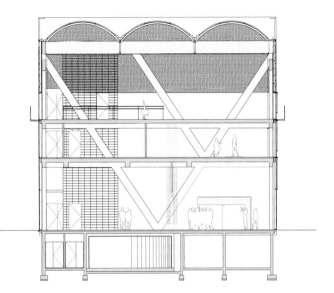

A section

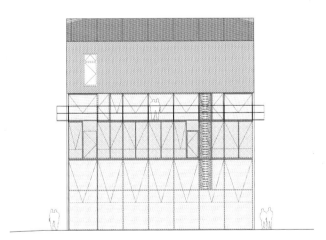

South elevation

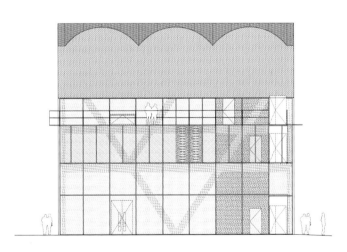

East elevation

MRI: New Generation Research Center

The New Generation Research Center (MRI is the acronym taken from its French moniker) takes part in the urban renewal of the peninsula of Caen. In a quickly changing territory that is punctuated by a collection of autonomous architecture, the project is a free-standing object. The same can be said of both its program and its architecture. Reinterpreting the storage shed, it deploys its program vertically, leaving the ground free and as circulation space.

The project indistinctly superimposes a public square, an exhibition space, a conference area, a bar, manufacturing workshops, a business incubator, and a generous event space on the roof; habitability at its maximum. A prefabricated and efficient structure generates free, flexible, and evolving platforms.

In its thirty meters of height, the building creates two types of spaces: the *plan libre* and the servings spaces, which include storage, sanitary facilities, and vertical circulations. Connected by a separate vertical structure that contains the elevators and the staircase, the three platforms float above the ground. Although contained in the same shell-like structure, the three platforms can operate independently, day or night.

This spatial organization gives the building the ability to respond to different programs' demands, which can change and evolve with time. Temporarily partitioned, configured, and re-configured, it creates new spaces and subspaces. It is a big playground.

Like a Swiss Army knife, the New Generation Research Center provides multiple functions in a rational and compact volume.

The MRI building was the winner of the Équerre d'Argent 2016 prize in the «Activities site» category.

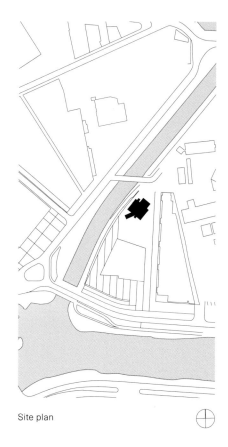

Site plan

DATE: 2013-2015 / LOCATION: Caen, France / BUILT AREA: 2,500 m² – 26,910 sf / PROGRAM: New Generation Sciences Center Peninsula Caen / CLIENT: Association Relais d'sciences / STATUS: Completed, won competition entry / DESIGN TEAM: Bruther / COLLABORATORS: Inex, Bmf, Altia, Aia Management, Batiserf / PHOTOS: Maxime Delvaux (p. 150, p. 152, p. 156, p. 159), Filip Dujardin (p. 160), Julien Hourcade (p. 149)

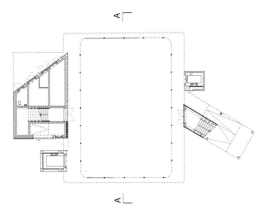

Ground floor

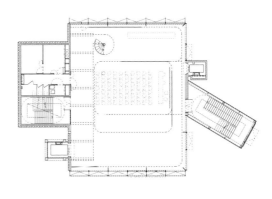

First floor

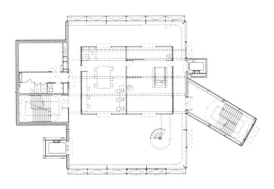

Second floor

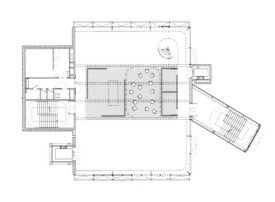

Third floor

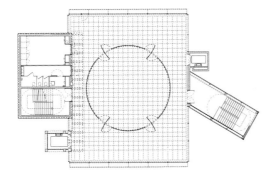

Fourth floor

"The project indistinctly superimposes a public square, an exhibition space, a conference area, a bar, manufacturing workshops, a business incubator, and a generous event space on the roof; habitability at its maximum."

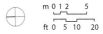

Functionality options

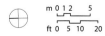

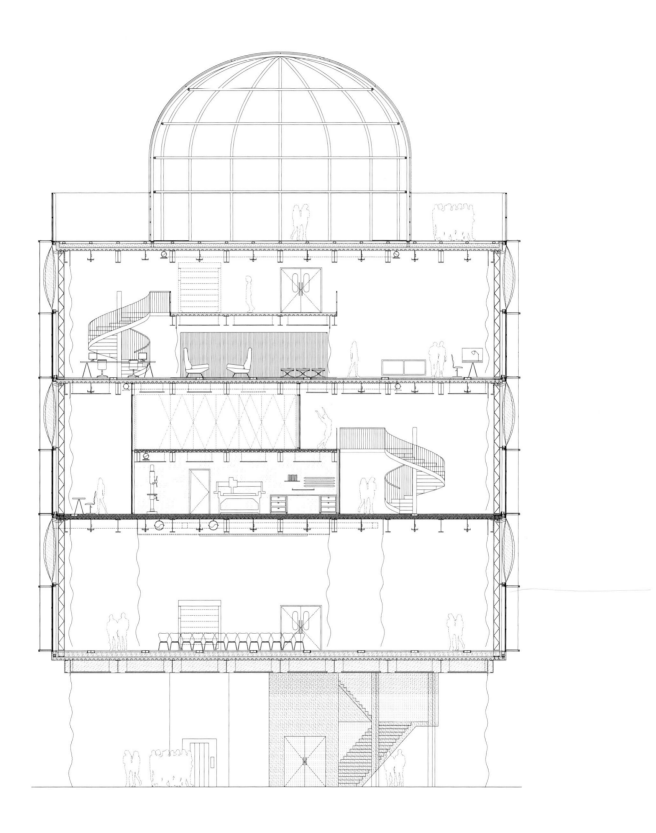

A section

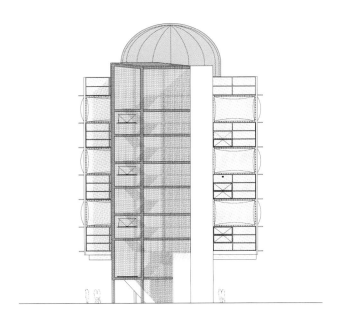

Southeast elevation

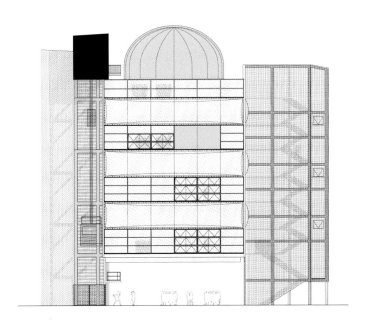

Northeast elevation

NAVIRE URBAIN

J'ai longé le canal pour te rejoindre. J'ai traversé le pont du rendez-vous. Évidemment, tu n'y étais pas. À l'horizon était amarré un navire, familier et énigmatique à la fois. Son étrange proue a surgi depuis la rue. Alors je me suis approché de cet objet trouvé, mirage au milieu d'un océan de réalité. Si ses contours changeaient sans cesse à mesure de mes pas, je me souviens de son dôme qui découpait le ciel.

Ainsi commençait cette croisière improvisée dans une mer laide et magnifique, banale et exceptionnelle. Depuis le quai, le bateau semblait flotter au-dessus du sol. En avançant davantage, j'ai découvert le dispositif, la structure préfabriquée, sa grande capacité, les situations qu'elle permettait, les espaces complémentaires et potentiels. J'ai fait escale dans chacun des plateaux libres, flexibles et évolutifs - sans doute était-ce la plus grande aire de jeux imaginable. Ils offraient la promesse d'une habitabilité maximale. Tout devenait alors possible.

Dans le ventre de la machine, j'ai trouvé un microcosme. Les rencontres, les idées, les rêves même, convergeaient vers ce cargo peuplé d'investisseurs, de chercheurs et de visiteurs. J'ai vu un réceptacle m'embarquer du sol au ciel dans un voyage immobile. J'ai observé la ville du haut de mon promontoire. Je me suis dit que l'on vivrait bien, ici.

Et puis le phare s'est illuminé à la tombée de la nuit. J'ai quitté le bateau et les songes en suspension dans l'espace. J'ai retrouvé la rumeur de la ville en imaginant mon prochain départ à bord du navire. Je savais que, si je passais le pont et regagnais son ciel, il m'emmènerait où je voulais.

Rue Pelleport

This social housing building is situated in a typical Parisian context in the 20th district. The near-built landscape is inter-mixed with impressive adjoining buildings from the seventies; the project is built in a traversing plot parcel between two streets in a very dense urban fabric. However, the project re-establishes the street alignment and explores the urban possibilities for shaping the contiguous lots, generating a dialogue between those singular domestic architectures.

Due to local urban plan regulations, the main geometry is composed of two vertical prisms linked by a central building that is oriented toward a garden. This composition grants several typologies of housing units sharing a common circulation principle. Except for the studio, all of the units have a double east-west orientation with generous exterior spaces that allow natural light all day long. The volumetric fragmentation of the project creates a diverse typology in which each housing unit acquires a unique view and relationship to its environment.

The courtyard is at the heart of the lot, it is a quiet and intimate place that creates generous space for the building's inhabitants to enjoy. Covered or opened to the sky, it can be turned into a garden, a bike garage, or a playground. To both preserve intimacy and protect against the sun, the project uses three types of material to generate filters: natural anodized aluminum, colored fabric curtains, and glass. The façades react to the game of light and shadow and reveal an abstract structure.

In spite of the small size of the lot and specific demands of the social housing program, the project creates generous spaces and unique individual units.

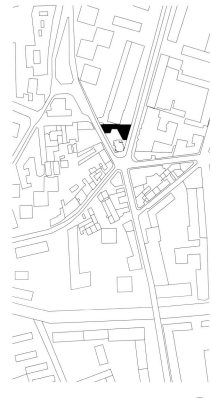

Site plan

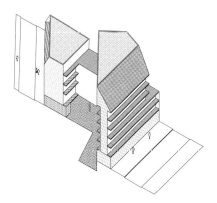

DATE: 2009-2017 / LOCATION: 133-135 rue Pelleport, Paris 20th, France / BUILT AREA: 1,850 m² – 19,913 sf / PROGRAM: 25 social housing units and a commercial space / CLIENT: SIEMP / STATUS: Completed, won competition entry / DESIGN TEAM: Bruther / COLLABORATORS: Louis Choulet (Environmental and fluids engineer), 12 Eco (Economist), EVP (Structure engineer), SBG Lutèce (General contractor) / PHOTOS: Maxime Delvaux (p. 169 top), Julien Hourcade (p. 163, p. 164, p. 166, p. 167, p. 169 bottom)

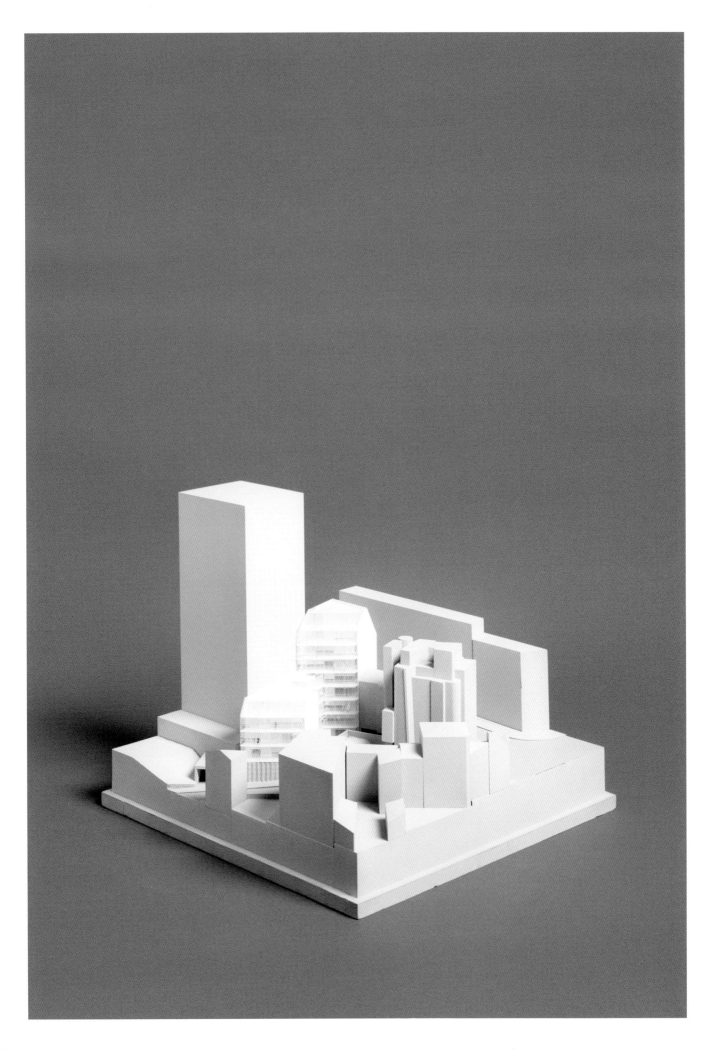

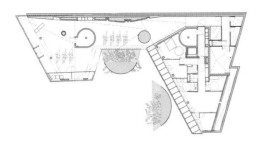

Ground floor

First floor

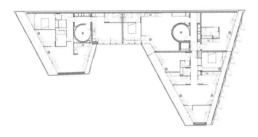

Second floor

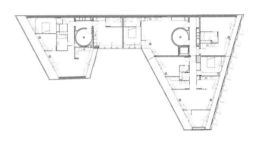

Third floor

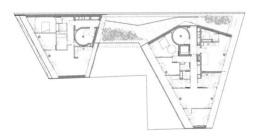

Fourth floor

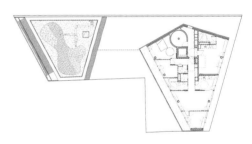

Fifth floor

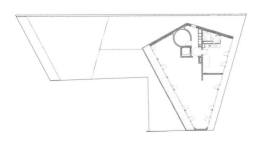

Sixth floor

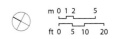

m 0 1 2　　5
ft 0　5　10　20

"The volumetric fragmentation of the project creates a diverse typology in which each housing unit acquires a unique view and relationship to its environment."

Section

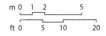

L'ESCALE

Cher A,

Depuis hier, nous surplombons la ville.
Le panorama est à couper le souffle. La nuit est calme et ses
lumières douces nous laissent présager un futur radieux. Nous
apercevons au loin les toits mythiques, couchés sur le dos avec
leurs petites pattes en l'air, la quiétude métropolitaine et les
emblèmes d'un nouveau monde qui semble avoir toujours été là.
Mais je ne vais pas vous barber avec une longue description ici.
Entre nous, personne ne lit les longues descriptions barbantes
jusqu'au bout. Quoi qu'il en soit, cette arrivée marque un nouveau
départ. Nous avons quitté la réalité immédiate et accablante. Nous
avons laissé derrière nous la pesanteur, l'inertie et l'opacité du
quotidien pour une escale infinie.

C'est ici que nous resterons.
Nous avons trouvé un refuge immuable en ce vaisseau de verre
posé au sommet de la montagne de zinc. L'ailleurs commence ici.
Nous pensons bien à vous depuis notre point de vue. Parfois, nous
nous plaisons à penser que vous apparaissez quelque part, là, dans
ce paysage mouvant que nous ne nous lassons pas de contempler.
Nous vous écrirons demain pour plus de détails. Quant à quitter la
ville, nous n'y pensons même plus.

Sciences de la Vie Building

Designing a new project for the EPFL site is very challenging. It must not only contend with the delicate balance of the landscape but also the great architecture works already on site. With projects from SANAA, Dominique Perrault, Kengo Kuma and Associates, and Office Kersten Geers David Van Severen, the site is a great playground for architectural excellence and calls upon architects to assert their own vision. The ground implantation strategy is a pragmatic response to the site's condition; it is pursued in the building's structural logic. On its east side, the site works within a large 'infrastructure' system, using a gateway to distribute and connect the buildings. On its west side, it uses a 'campus' logic based on speared pavilions. To reconcile these two systems, the building is located at the end of the major distribution axis and asserts itself as a new autonomous pavilion.

The building has to contend with two specific program requirements. The first deals with requests related to the practical work of students in biology and chemistry; the second is about investigation and research activities in neuroscience and fundamental microbiology. Common areas, relaxation spaces, and conference rooms complete the program. Compactness, functionality, and flexibility are the architects' response to those requirements. Playing with this density, circulations are established within a concentric organization that moves from the 'black boxes of labs' in the center, to the vast 'transparent crown' in the periphery, giving the idea of a 'foliated prism' view from the outside.

A system of peripheral walkways draws attention to the natural light. The relationship between inside and outside favors the consciousness of the immediate environment. This almost complete transparency of the first layer of the project conjures up one of the program's original constraints, a large number of spaces without light.

The building possesses six floors at its center and three double heights in its periphery, which allow for an extension of working space in the form of mezzanines. The collective spaces, like the auditorium, the restaurant, and the café, are all grouped on the accessible roof terrace. These enclosed spaces are delimited by a roof made of repetitive sheds, which bring in a unique light.

The building becomes a hybrid organism with its own breath. It is a glazed pavilion, almost evanescent, which hides a real 'architectural machinery' at its center.

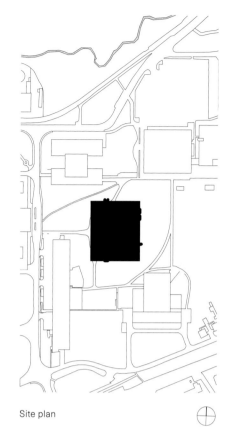

Site plan

DATE: 2016-2021 / LOCATION: University of Lausanne, Lausanne, Switzerland / BUILT AREA: 27,000 m² – 29,0625 sf / PROGRAM: New Faculty of Biology Building for the University of Lausanne (UNIL) and the École Polytechnique Fédérale de Lausanne (EPFL) / CLIENT: University of Lausanne / STATUS: Won competition entry / DESIGN TEAM: Bruther with BAUKUNST / PHOTOS: Maxime Delvaux, Julien Hourcade (p. 171)

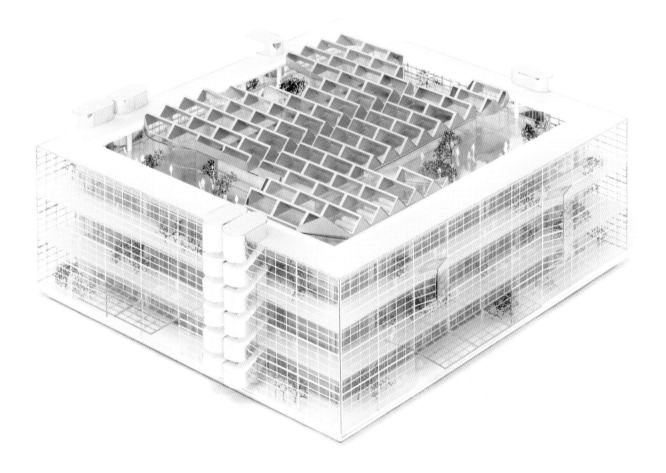

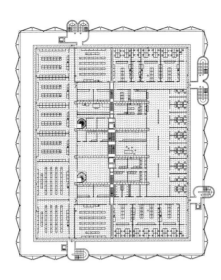

First floor

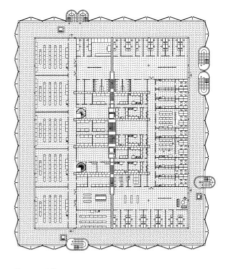

Second floor

Third floor

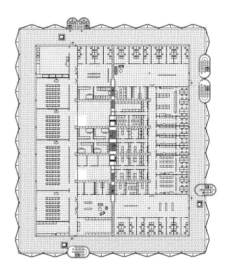

Fourth floor

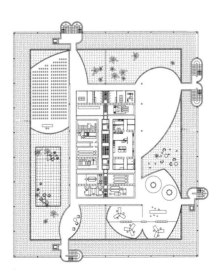

Fifth floor

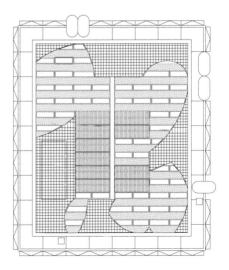

Roof plan

Coursive scheme

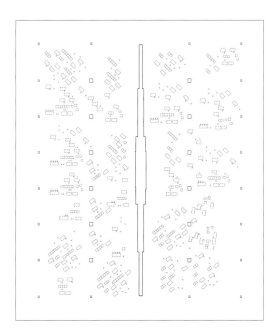

Flexibility scheme

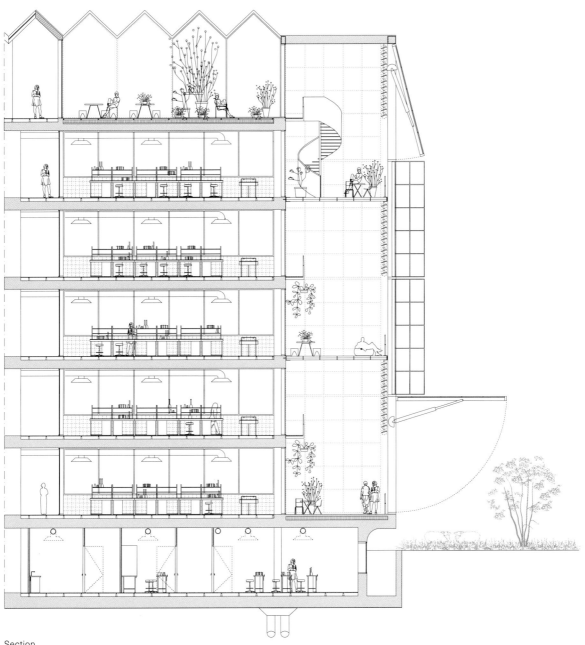

Section

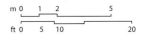

In 2008, Jing Liu and Florian Idenburg ran into each other on the streets of New York, a few years after their first meeting in Tokyo, when they were working for SANAA. That accidental encounter marked a turning point in their lives and the start of a very personal project. At the time, Idenburg was still connected to the Japanese practice, doing some U.S.-based projects and teaching at Harvard with Ryue Nishizawa, where Ilias Papageorgiou was his student. As they describe it, the three of them started to 'softly' leave their previous jobs, to open SO – IL, Solid Objectives. Together they would find a unique—and consistent—mode of understanding architecture.

SO – IL

Pole Dance concept diagram. MoMA PS1, New York, 2010.

Multiple Narratives

Florencia Rodriguez interviews Jing Liu and Ilias Papageorgiou at their office in New York.

Last summer we had the opportunity to visit SO – IL and sit down with Liu and Papageorgiou to discuss their practice and experiences. Later that day, they would present their first monographic book: "Solid Objectives: Order, Edge, Aura" at the New Museum. The editing process had brought them to a very analytical point in their growing career. As we discovered in our conversation, their propensity for staking out new territory stands out as one of their most important qualities.

TO SAY SOMETHING

FLORENCIA RODRIGUEZ
I have always been curious about the name of the office. Why SO – IL?

JING LIU
We started the office nine years ago, but I can recall the impulse quite accurately, so the way I am going to be talking about it is somewhat reflective. Florian and I were both in New York at the time but had worked and studied in Europe and Asia before. We were teaching here and felt bewildered that the academy and the practice—or maybe the profession—were so far apart [...] There was such a huge divide that it felt rather unnecessary to be there.
At the same time, there was a great financial crisis and everyone was talking about technological disruption. Since we had previously worked in the post-bubble Japan, it seemed very natural that something would happen as things were exploding. Things were going in all different directions. Those are moments in which you can grab what is in the air and start solidifying it, to work on a new state of things, so we named the office Solid Objectives. We were (and are still) not very sure if the name should have been derived from our names or an agenda, because each speaks to a very different way of practice. We thought at first—this is a very personal effort and that shouldn't be hidden behind something abstract—but, at the same time, we should not be afraid of claiming that this was a

search for something that could be larger than ourselves. So we invented a new word.
SO – IL is a word that has an awareness of itself: it resembles something universal and material while referring both to something personal and something beyond the personal. So, I guess that was our impulse to start the office: solidifying the bits and pieces in 2008, capturing it in history, changing the state of things, bringing together our searches by charging the conversation with another narrative and a new imagination.

FR   Before formally starting this conversation, we were talking about Marx's definition of modernism as these solids that melt into air; I feel there is a connection between that idea and what you have just explained. Does this mean that you were criticizing modernity—or a form of modernism— or are you talking about just another turn of the state of the arts that you wanted to reflect? What was it that was finishing?

JL   I think the Marxian revolution is not yet finished. It needs to be examined as a discourse in a new context and we need to define what we need to destroy and what we want to inherit from modernity. Modernity shouldn't be destroyed. There was an inevitable reason for it to be part of human history, and it led us to globalism and liberalism, which are causing us a lot of pain now. But it also inspired a vibrant cultural conversation and very productive political discussions. Globalism has vividly exposed to us how that conversation was siloed in a very narrow way, and scattered unevenly. Now we see that different regions in the world lived in their own versions of the modern narrative and they are not all compatible with each other. In China, for example, our experience of modernism is very different from that of the West. It's warped, it has the propensity to be explosive and authoritarian, and it is intensely material. The Great Leap Forward and the Cultural Revolution left us so deprived that liberalization was not just a fix, it was a matter of life or death. So, our tolerance with globalization and liberalization should be understood in this context. Now it seems we have no choice but to talk to each other and try to understand what the same thing means to one other.

Ilias is from Greece for instance, and the Mediterranean narrative is very different from that of Continental Europe. There are frictions, incompatibilities, and misunderstandings between these narratives that have to coexist. We might be talking about the same thing, but our experience of it is vastly different.

And this is something that we want to reflect on—this political, cultural, and material part of modernism in today's context. We use many different words to describe what we are trying to do in a very fluid and intuitive way, we use terms like ambiguity and androgynous modernity, we talk about a condition that is blurred and indeterminate, but they all more or less point to the same thing.

FR   Which project was the first that you think consolidated the practice as 'a practice,' as SO – IL's practice?

JL   I would say Pole Dance, MoMA PS1. I think PS1 was the one for which we were propelled to have a story about what we were trying to do. When you start an office, no one is there waiting for you to tell them what you are trying to do. But because the platform of PS1 is such an important one—both in the arts and in academia—and because we won the competition basically in our first year, we were immediately put on the spot, having to explain to people why we were there. I think that resonated with people and we also realized that the way people talked about it and how they reflected on the structure itself was much richer than what we had imagined. Of course, we wanted to talk about technology, we wanted to talk about flexibility and elasticity, we wanted to talk about play, but the fact that people were engaging with it in such a visceral and direct fashion—it acted as the physical metaphor for a technological reality. That was very touching. It was like bringing abstraction into something physical and tangible, so that one can interact and play with it.

ILIAS PAPAGEORGIOU
        It was really interactive, basically.

JL   Some people were just happy that they could hang on it and play with it in such an unconstrained way. There's no apparent rule to the play, you can do whatever you want but then you are confronted with the elasticity of the system and you realize quickly enough that you can actually destroy it, which is how our relationship with our environment and our humanity works. In the installation, they would confront the responsibility that individuals have to the larger system. Of course, all these ideas are not new, but it was very powerful to have the physical dimension and the physical space to be the mediator. That made us more convinced about working in the medium of architecture, and with physical space in particular.

At the same time, we were working on the project for Kukje Gallery, which took much longer but implied the same things—the physical form, labor, and experience in a global and liberalized world. It also confirmed to us that we need to stick to buildings, space, and objects, and use the material and tactile reality of architecture as a way to communicate and experiment, and eventually, maybe, transform.

FR   I was just about to ask you something about that because many of the projects—even when you look at the pictures—transmit something about that kind of experience. You immediately feel that there is something about this haptic experience of the object ... You really want to go and try to touch the building and have this physical relation that you are inviting us to have with the space. What did this first project give back to you?

IP   What was very important from the beginning when we started to think about this project was to create an experience, an environment. We didn't want to just put an object in the courtyard that the visitor would just look at. We wanted to offer an experience at all levels—and definitely a sensorial one; so, there was this idea of the fabric, and the shadows and lights became very important to this intention of immersing the visitor into an environment.

Another thing that was quite important, to continue the previous conversation, is the idea of openness, which I think also relates to your question earlier on modernity where there was a quest for the perfection, the perfect final state. In PS1 there is no final state. This is an environment that always evolves with the interactions of its users.

But also it was quite amazing how being basically a piece of infrastructure, it created other projects that we had not foreseen from the beginning: we had a performance component with pole dancers that danced in the installation, a sound piece which we worked with ARUP Acoustics, and we developed a drawing and real-time volume control app with 2x4.

Ph: Miguel de Guzmán / ImagenSubliminal

COCOONING

FR   Then, going back to this idea of thinking about a turning point, there appears to be something about questioning the discipline in your explanations. All these other projects are already saying that there is more to it than the classic closed object.

I have the image of the Kukje Gallery in my mind and the fact that there are those different experiences between the outside and the inside takes me to your idea of interiority. In your recent book you have an interesting text about what you call 'Cocooning,'[1] could you talk a little bit about that?

JL   I think the way Japanese architecture is reflected on urbanism with the idea that urban space can be understood as interior space was very relevant to this project. Creating private territories in the public domain and hosting private thoughts is very important to us. I would say that the reason I wanted to work for Sejima was really because she stood out to me as making a kind of interiority that was very much speaking to the ethos of this hyper-urban condition, a kind of interiority that was privately open. It does not overtly project outwards, and yet, because of this protected privacy, it engages seductively. There is something really elegant and fluid in the spaces she creates.

Our formal approach, the material experience that we are looking for, and the way we are making things—say, techniques—are very different from her work. But what we learned from her is this disposition towards urban context as an interior space.

Breathe – MINI Living, one of our latest installations, acts in a similar fashion. It is nested in an alley, which is already a kind of interior space, and then creates an object that is outwardly projective (to a degree) but is also encapsulating a world within itself. Kukje Gallery was nested in the oldest neighborhood in Korea, with the Imperial Palace right across the street. It is also nested within the courtyard houses around it. As a contemporary art gallery, we had to make an abstract void in there. So, do you drop it in and erase a certain part of the city? Or can the void also project something outward? How can we flip the inside outside?

If we think of the urban context as already part of the interior, then the 'void' is the other interior that is inside of it. There is a very interesting spatial relationship in that.

FR   And there is something about the mesh that also works like a buffer between that interior, the city and this kind of space that you were describing.

IP   I think in both of these examples there is also this other space in a way that is neither inside nor outside but more like an in-between zone. And I think this in-between zone is interesting, in Kukje Gallery, between the mesh and the wall, one gets through all these different layers and boundaries.

FR   That's interesting, and I see a lot of that also at the Manetti Shrem Museum of Art, for instance.

So, going back to the role of the architect, where do you think we are going or, where are we standing?

JL   Well, I think this idea of the narrative is something very different in our generation. We are not ideological anymore, the singular idea that everyone has to get behind is gone. And so, we choose to work on the spatial, the material, and the structural, creating a carrier of multiple conversations. It could still have a very strong formal inclination and directionality but is open to many interpretations. If someone wants to do a pole dance show in here because that is what it triggers in them, great! Architecture can be very generous in that sense.

I think that is the beauty of architecture. Architecture spans over many decades, sometimes centuries. Before the interview, we were talking about language, and how words can be redefined so many times in history. Architectural language works in the same way but even more fluidly. We do not need to prescribe rigidly what it is now, but to craft a strong directionality that embodies broadly how we feel about our common space and our private spaces, and where we want to take the conversation. This way, architecture can be liberated to serve a broader audience and many generations to come.

FR   You mention the popularity of TEDx talks in one of your texts and many other things that are circulating so fluidly.[2] At the same time, we are constantly listening or reading about the relevance of design innovation. The porosity of these breathing objects that you are proposing, are, in a way, pushing the meanings of interiority/exteriority, architecture/urbanism. They are statements in themselves, even though they are not shouting aloud.

JL   Yes, we were hoping to find a way for architecture space and experience to be critical in and of itself, rather than creating architectural criticism as a separate discourse.

FR   Avoiding the idea of a discourse that you overlap it with...

JL   With Kukje Gallery, basically you weave through a network of narrow alleyways and maybe you catch a glimpse of this somewhat strange looking thing. Then you are suddenly up against it, and the enormity of its craft—500,000 rings hand-welded together. It is not something that you expect to find in a historical neighborhood like this, so it confronts you with the oddity of its situation. It confronts you with the reversal of interior and exterior, future and history—similar to that of Pole Dance. How can you make architectural experience critical? So that we as users and occupants will interact with it in a critical way? I think that is ultimately what we are trying to do. Ultimately, words are not our tool of communication, we want to revive architecture as a form of language that can become more self-aware and critical in and of itself.

FR   As a mode of thought, also.

JL   Yes, exactly.

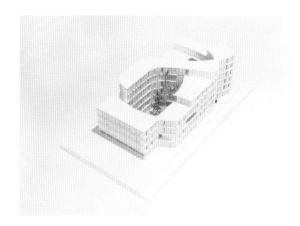

Housing in León, Mexico. Aerial view of the model.

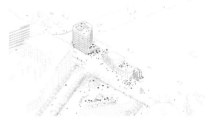

Place Mazas – Réinventer la Seine, Paris, 2017.
SO – IL & laisné roussel
Competition winning project

L'Atelier de l'Arsenal projects the riverfront transformation of the underused site of Place Mazas into a new social node for Paris including a housing program with shared spaces for the residents as well as public activities.

FR   And what is new in your current projects? What can we expect of them?

JL   Place Mazas, the project in Paris, is a good illustration of architectural practice moving towards a much more collaborative model. In this project, developers, social scientists, architects, engineers, and community workers work as one team with a single vision, which they pitch to the city.
So rather than the architect's formal agenda alone, the activist's social agenda alone, or the developer's economic agenda alone, it is a socialized agenda. This way of working definitely generates a lot of frictions along the way, but I think we can afford to do so in our society, and if we are all committed to it, the result can be great. I am on the board of Van Alen Institute,[3] which is a non-profit organization very much pushing this kind of interdisciplinary conversation. In getting policy makers, designers, and communities together, the process changes the outcome. I do think that substantial change requires many people to be involved and engaged.

IP   I believe we are always thinking about the urban and the city, even when we work with objects or smaller installations. Even with Kukje Gallery one might say, "Oh, this is beautiful, nice!" but I think the idea really comes from thinking about the urban. In this project in Paris we are trying to work with larger scales and with more complex components. It is about designing at the intersection of development, programming, and community, and how with the proposal, we are orchestrating all the components implied in the urban.

FR   Is it the first project of that scale?

JL   No, we have other projects under construction of similar scale and complexity. There's a project in Brooklyn that also works in the neighborhood scale and another project under construction in Hong Kong that has a lot to do with the mixed-use context, the dirty and messy urbanism.
In the beginning, we were reacting to certain things and happenings around us and trying to use architecture as a tool to push back against a certain reality. Now we are transitioning to a phase of using it as a tool to build. We have stirred up certain imaginations, the question now is how to translate it to many people who are not exposed to architecture when the visual language they are versed in is very different from that of ours. There is much more we have to do to make architecture a common language that can be used to install new imaginations.

IP   I think what is interesting also, is how architecture can participate in shaping visions. This is the case for many of these projects, like the Brooklyn project that Jing mentioned, the Paris project, and I would even say, the Manetti Shrem Museum of Art, which is really a new institution that didn't exist before. As for the design, I think we also worked together with our clients to shape the vision and the mission of this project, because they did not exist. So, they were not typical projects, in which one responds to a brief and provides the square meters and the spaces for these problems, they were really more collaborative. We are not only architects providing spaces, we are also agents who shape the vision behind the project.

PRODUCTIVE MISUNDERSTANDINGS

FR   Do you think that being from three different countries and working in a fourth one, affects and forms that way of thinking?

JL & IP Definitely!

IP   And there are many more [countries] because the people who work with us, everyone is literally from a different place.

JL   Yes, we have to first overcome our own miscommunication and misinterpretation and then we have to convince each other—each of us are obviously very strong-minded and coming from great cultures. I'm talking about China, Greece, ancient civilizations, and New Amsterdam-New York, these are three very different cultural heritages. Imagine if you have to get the Greek, the Chinese, and the Dutch behind a single idea—it is a lot of work. [laughs]

IP   I think this confusion comes out in a way in the projects as a sense of providing a framework that can allow for these different interpretations, readings, experiences, to come out—because that is how it works.

FR   That is interesting, to think that misunderstanding and misinterpretations and translations in fact generate opportunities to think in a new way; they are productive.

JL   We always talk of taking risks. In America, everything is so risk-averse in practice and reckless in reality. It's all talk about liabilities and insurance. Architecture needs to be more intelligent in taking productive risks, otherwise nothing new can come out of it. Risk is a necessary part of creativity, and should be a necessary part of making architecture. That is why play is often part of our narrative. Let's be playful. There has to be a certain common trust and a sense of excitement for the unknown to be there.

IP   And that is something further intensified by the digital and the virtual. Through the internet, we found the manufacturer for Kukje Gallery, but when we went there it was the lowest tech ever…low-skill craftsmen making things by hand in a small village, which was actually really amazing.

FR   I really like this idea of 'making' that you are putting on the table and I would like you to talk a little more of your take on technology. Technology seems crucial to your project, but at the same time it is not on the front page.

JL   In the same way that we are trying to use architecture as a critical language, we are also trying to understand making as a thinking process. Ideas don't just come to you when you sit and look out into the sky, they can also come as you work on things. It's the traditional craftsmen's idea. You think through making, the hands and mind work together. So, if we understand technology as a thinking process, parametric as the way our brain works, with near infinite possibilities, materials can create boundaries and commonality. We use parametric design tools on a daily basis but we are not using them to generate finite forms, but as a thinking process. We test how that thinking process can direct the different ways our hands move and vice versa. It is this feedback loop that is very interesting to us.

FR   So, technology is a way of thinking about things. In which projects have you applied this way of scripting?

JL   Probably in every project.

IP   I think it is a lot about the thinking, parametricism is not about the tool. And I think technology is also not static, but something that constantly evolves. Architecture has such a long tradition and history of making, and the tools always changed with technology. The most interesting designs come when you are able to combine different tools. For example, for Davis (Manetti Shrem Museum of Art) the process of design of the canopy in the beginning was a kind of an intuitive model but then we also used scripting to—on one hand optimize the form of structure, and on the other hand, design the infill pattern to provide different light and shadow condition underneath. There, the parametric tool was very helpful in being able to calibrate different experiences underneath. The delivery was a designed-built process, so we had to fix a number to design within so that we could connect the design tool with the cost control of the project. Different concerns were interconnected, and they informed each other. It really helped us to be able to achieve this within these constraints.

FR   I guess sometimes art has the possibility of reflecting changes more instantly, and many of your projects are related to art. Is that something you looked for? Do you feel that you think as artists?

JL   Some of these things we were talking about is what artists are trying to do as well. So, I think it was definitely a very productive partnership, especially in the beginning, when we were searching. We were often thinking together, and pushing each other, because we are dealing with the same questions, although the mediums and audience are very different. So, I think it is just natural that with curators, directors, and artists, we gravitate towards each other. We have reflected on this. In the past nine years, all of our clients were people who were trying to do more or less the same thing as us but within their field. Either as a developer, a movie director, or a museum. We are also not working with just any museums, but often new museums or a new chapter in the history of an established one. But going back to your question of our next phase, I think we need not be so comfortable, we need to go out. Actually, we already have gone out and found out how difficult it is to do so. Not everyone has the same quest and ambition. We realized that there are completely different sets of problems and priorities.

Take affordability for instance—we are working on a few housing projects. We have done very little housing until now but our heart has always been there from the beginning. But we realized early on how difficult it is in today's market economy. We are going into construction on a vertical urban housing project in Leon, Mexico. Over the last twenty years, in Mexico, all the low-income housing projects were made like matchboxes, sprawled outside the city. But they have realized that this is completely unsustainable. There is no infrastructure, hours out of the city, there is no school, sometimes no sewage, and people need to pick up their own trash. But after a few decades, people are fixated with the idea that if they buy a house, it has to sit on the land. How to reverse that thinking both for the city and for the buyers? How can we make a project of vertical urban typology that appeals to people by giving them a different but much higher quality of life? So, we are trying to find a way of cracking the nut of a completely different set of problems here. We are feeling comfortable engaging with them, as opposed to a few years ago.

MAKING AS A PROCESS

FR   That is really interesting: it implies not being passive towards this other world of decision-making, getting involved, and generating the tools to think about it.

JL   In the project for Paris there was a very clear collective decision-making process not to build a huge building, but to provide public space.

IP   It happened both with Paris and the project for León, where design plays an important role.
      In the case of León, it was a tool to really convince the people that they can actually change their lifestyle and live in this vertical typology that is always so much more connected to the exterior: there are courtyards, there are shared spaces.
      And similarly, in Paris, the project is in one of the most prominent sites: in the city's intersection of Bastille axis with the river. It is part of Haussmann's plan and the site is a public monument, not a private development lot. There are other urban transformations coming in the future. For instance, there will be a new waterfront; Paris will be

removing the cars from the river's border.
      We understand that the city evolves, and that we should not just think about the current moment and place a building there, but rather how that space can become a key to the life of the city. So, we proposed much less volume than any of the other competitors. This approach is also related to an economical model of deposit, in which, due to the close collaboration with the developer, we were able to make it work. We left part of the site as a leased property, activating it during that time and then working with the city again in, say, 15-20 years. Together with the city, there will be another opportunity to evaluate what to do with the place. It is urban design.

JL   I think that what we were able to bring to the table was the idea that public spaces and their history are collectively owned by the people. We understand and support the idea that things need to change and the market needs to work to make things flow. But change can be balanced and considered, we don't need to turn public assets immediately into private ones. That's what we have been doing over the last decades. In doing so, we tend to make problems that we then need to solve immediately after. But if we generally believe public amenity is important, you can get some capital and make only the necessary densification. Then in ten years, when the surroundings have changed, and the market has changed, there is another opportunity to redefine the relationship between the public and private.

IP   I think there is also something interesting about the synergy between the public and the private domain. When you have to talk to the people, the case needs to make sense for them, it's not only making it look cool for the politicians or to pocket big profit for a few people. And in my opinion what is great about the process Paris is having is that it transforms even the developers and their thinking, because they have to compete with each other on ideas and work in those terms.

FR   During the conversation, the idea of the project as something that transcends the object came out repeatedly, making it clearer to understand how you transform this mode of thought that we were talking about at the beginning, into form. How does the idea of wrapping work in those terms?

IP   There is something in the quality that is really hard to describe. It can be sharp, it can be curved, it can be smooth. The lightness is never defined so there is no sharp shadow. It is like creating this form that can be read in many different ways but cannot be described. It is also really hard to draw with traditional architectural conventions.

Ph: Courtesy of Iwan Baan. Storefront for Art and Architecture.

Blueprint at Storefront for Art and Architecture, New York, 2015. SO – IL and Sebastiaan Bremer.

SO – IL's installation shrink-wraps the gallery's façade of varied and irregular openings, transforming the existing exterior into one continuous and undulating surface.

JL   The wrapping is a line that you can never draw. It's not just the architects drawing a line and getting it built: it is a process. With wrapping you need to have the volume there first, like with Kukje Gallery or what we did at the Storefront. The program or the spaces exist before and the wrap holds them together.

We make models and we draw sections and we script them but we know that the final result is not going to be that. We are not trying to control the line; we are trying to approximate. It's a process. And that is actually the beauty of doing things with your hands because you try to make something, and maybe it does not work well and your hand must adjust to that, and then you add a bit more tension or you relax a little bit, right?

The beauty of thinking with your hands, in a way, is exactly that—knowing when to relax. You just don't have to resolve everything in your head.

IP   In that sense, it is also because we now say that with parametric and digital fabrication, you can have all these unique objects. It is not about the mechanical reproduction of modernism or creating an identical copy. It is not about copies. And that, I think, maybe relates more with the notion that the handmade and the manual can never be identical. They are similar but there is never an identical copy. That is where these two relate.

FR   Indeterminacy or uncertainty, but not in a skeptical way; more as a symbol of openness to possibilities, to things you cannot imagine or synthesize … Sounds like life!

1   SO – IL: Florian Idenburg, Jing Liu, Ilias Papageorgiou. "Cocooning" in: "Solid Objectives: Order, Edge, Aura." Zürich: Lars Müller Publishers, 2017.
2   SO – IL: Florian Idenburg, Jing Liu, Ilias Papageorgiou. "Learning curves" in: "Solid Objectives: Order, Edge, Aura." Zürich: Lars Müller Publishers, 2017.
3   Van Alen Institute, New York. www.vanalen.org

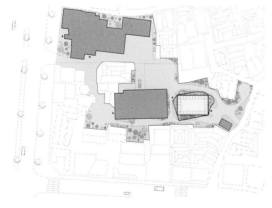

Site plan

DATE: April 2012 / LOCATION: Seoul, South Korea / BUILT AREA: 1,500 m² - 16,000 sf / CLIENT: Kukje Gallery / PROGRAM: gallery, theater, meeting room, art storage / STATUS: Completed / RECOGNITION: 2011 AIA NY Design Awards / TEAM: Florian Idenburg, Jing Liu, Ilias Papageorgiou, Iannis Kandyliaris, Cheon-Kang Park, Sooran Kim / FAÇADE ENGINEER: Front, Inc. / LOCAL ARCHITECT: Jong-Ga Architects / STRUCTURAL ENGINEER: Dong Yang Engineering / MEP: G.K Technology / PHOTOS: Iwan Baan

Kukje Gallery

For this art building in Seoul, SO – IL has developed a master plan of the gallery's art campus in the historic urban fabric of Sogyeok-dong, a low-rise area in the northern part of Seoul. Small alleyways and courtyard houses characterize this neighborhood, which is currently being infiltrated by newly constructed galleries, boutiques, and coffee shops.

One of the newly planned buildings within the master plan is SO – IL's gallery. Considering the clear diagrammatic geometry of the white cube too rigid within the historic fabric, the building is enveloped in a permanent 'nebula'—a pliable chainmail veil. The stainless steel mesh produces a layer of diffusion in front of the actual building mass, through a combination of multidirectional reflection, openness, and the *moiré* pattern generated through interplay of its shadows. The layering technique provides that the building with an inherently closed program looks fascinating during both day and night. It allows for a highly flexible white box gallery by placing circulation on the perimeter. An additional quality of the material is that it can stretch, thus avoiding creasing. It is strong, yet pliable, and can easily wrap around crude geometries. The structure is a single-story, clear-span art space. A perimeter skylight admits and diffuses natural light. The ground floor is used for large installations, performances and other functions, while the two sublevel floors house a sixty-seat dark-stained wood-clad auditorium, administrative areas, catering spaces, restrooms, and mechanical spaces.

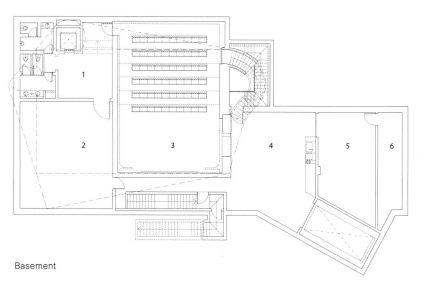

Basement

1   Lobby - Reception
2   Office - Lounge
3   Theater
4   Preparing room
5   Elevator controls
6   Pump

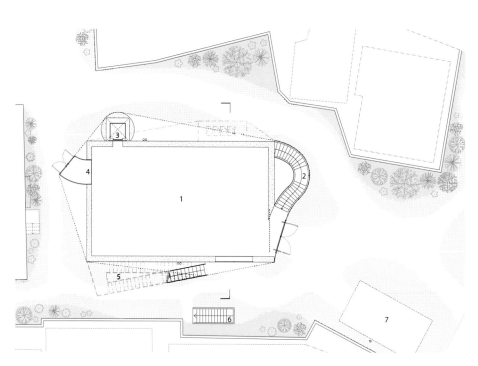

Ground floor

1   Gallery
2   Stairs to basement / storage
3   Elevator
4   Lobby
5   Stairs to roof top
6   Exit
7   Car elevator

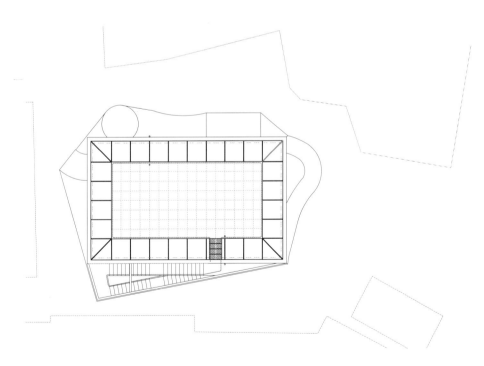

Roof Plan

m 0 1 2   5
ft 0   5   10   20

"We had to make an abstract void in Seoul's oldest neighborhood. So, do you drop it in and erase a certain part of the city? Or can the void also project something outward? How can we flip the inside outside? If we think of the urban context as already part of the interior, then the 'void' is the other interior that is inside of it." JL

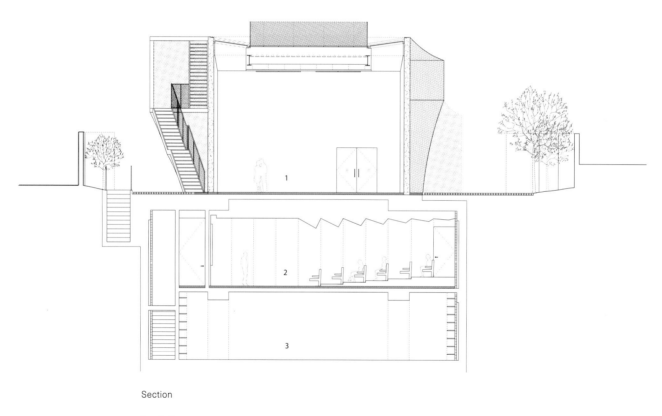

Section

1   Gallery
2   Theater
3   Basement / Storage

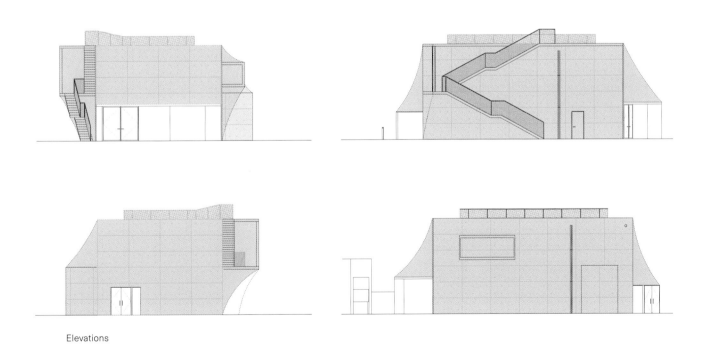

Elevations

m 0 1 2   5

ft 0   5   10   20

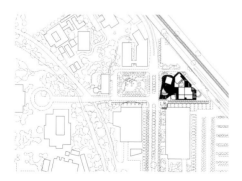

Site plan

DATE: Competition entry, 2013, First Prize; Completed 2016 / LOCATION: Davis, USA / BUILT AREA: 2,700 m² – 29,000 sf / PROGRAM: Museum of art / CLIENT: University of California, Davis / STATUS: Completed / TEAM: COMPETITION: Florian Idenburg, Ilias Papageorgiou, Jing Liu, Danny Duong, Seunghyun Kang, Nile Greenberg, Pietro Pagliaro, Andre Herrero, Madelyn Ringo, Jacopo Lugli / REALISATION: Florian Idenburg, Ilias Papageorgiou, Jing Liu, Danny Duong, Kevin Lamyuktseung / COLLABORATORS: ASSOCIATE ARCHITECT: Bohlin Cywinski Jackson / CONTRACTOR: Whiting-Turner / STRUCTURAL ENGINEER: Rutherford & Chekene / MECHANICAL ENGINEER: WSP / SUSTAINABILITY: WSP / LIGHTING: Fisher Marantz Stone / CANOPY ENGINEER: Front Inc. / PHOTOS: Iwan Baan

Jan Shrem and Maria

Manetti Shrem Museum of Art

The Museum captures the spirit of the California Central Valley: the empowerment of being able to cultivate and grow freely, and a sense of optimism, imagination, and invention. As an overarching move, a 50,000 square-foot permeable cover—a 'Grand Canopy'—extends over both site and building. The distinct shape of this open roof presents a new symbol for the campus. The Canopy blurs the edges of the site, creating a sensory landscape of activities and scales.

Like the Central Valley, the landscape under the Canopy becomes shaped and activated by changing light and seasons. Its unique form engenders curiosity from a distance, like a lone hill on a skyline. Interwoven curved and straight sections seamlessly define inside and outside. The result is a portfolio of interconnected interior and exterior spaces, all with distinct spatial qualities and characteristics that trigger diverse activities and create informal opportunities for learning and interaction.

The art museum is neither isolated nor exclusive, but open and permeable; it is not a static shrine, but a constantly evolving public event.

Plan - concept diagram

Ground floor

1	Gallery 1	6	Courtyard	11	Gallery custodial & storage	16	Volunteer lounge
2	Gallery 2	7	Building mechanical	12	Gallery mech	17	Community education
3	Gallery 3	8	Hall	13	Lobby	18	Service yard
4	Gallery 4	9	Open office	14	Coat storage	19	Art loading
5	Gallery 5	10	Art handling room	15	Boiler		

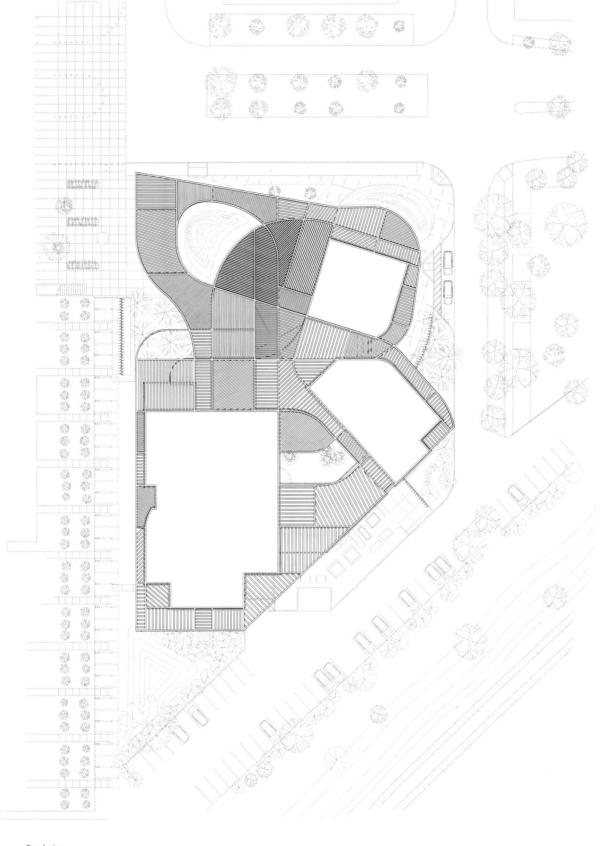

Roof plan

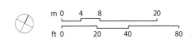

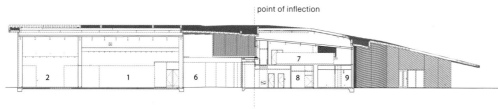

point of inflection

Section through gallery and office pavilion

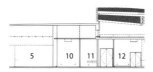

Section through gallery support

Section through restrooms and office pavilion

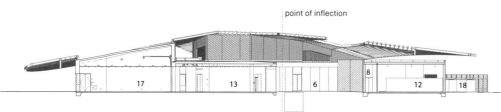

point of inflection

Section through education pavilion and support areas

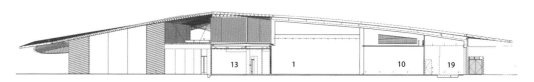

Section through gallery and support gallery

1	Gallery 1	6	Courtyard	11	Gallery custodial & storage	16	Volunteer lounge
2	Gallery 2	7	Building mechanical	12	Gallery mech	17	Community education
3	Gallery 3	8	Hall	13	Lobby	18	Service yard
4	Gallery 4	9	Open office	14	Coat storage	19	Art loading
5	Gallery 5	10	Art handling room	15	Boiler		

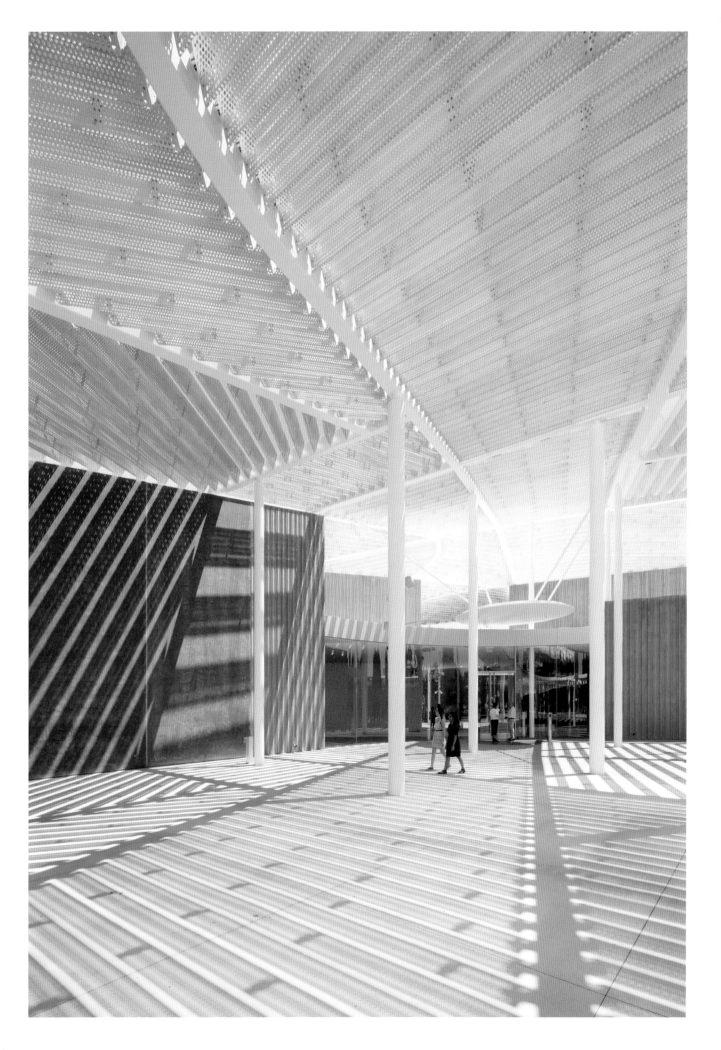

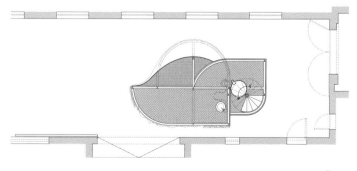

Site plan

DATE: April 2017 / LOCATION: Milan, Italy / BUILT AREA: 80 m² – 860 sf / PROGRAM: House prototype / CLIENT: MINI Living / STATUS: Completed / TEAM: Florian Idenburg, Jing Liu, Ilias Papageorgiou, Ian Ollivier, Isabel Sarasa Mené, Iason Houssein, Pietro Pagliaro, Alvaro Gomez Selles / COLLABORATORS: FABRICATOR: Xilografia Nuova Srl / PHOTOS: Laurian Ghinitoiu

Breathe – MINI Living

Breathe is a housing prototype for the future living environment that takes a holistic approach to sustainability. By making living an active experience, the installation shines a spotlight on environmental awareness and encourages visitors to confront the tendency to take resources for granted.

This house eschews a traditional organization with rooms dedicated to specific functions for a composition of a loose stack of porous realms. The incarnation for Salone del Mobile 2017 creates an attractive living area for up to three people on a previously unused 50-square-meter (538-square-feet) urban plot. A modular metal frame forms the basic structure of Breathe, and a flexible, light-permeable outer skin of purifying fabric creates the boundary between inside and outside. A total of six potential rooms and a roof garden provide space for domestic experience both collective and private. A variety of atmospheres are made through the manipulation of light, air, and water. Designed to be disassembled and reinstalled at other locations, the structure is mobile and adaptable. The fabric can be replaced to perform appropriately to a wide array of climates and environmental conditions.

MINI Living is an initiative launched in 2016 as a creative platform for MINI to develop architectural solutions for future urban living spaces. Last year, MINI Living showcased visionary concepts for shared and collaborative living/lifestyles/working in urban areas through the installations MINI Living – Do Disturb (at the Salone del Mobile in Milan) and MINI Living – Forests (at the London Design Festival). Breathe – MINI Living is the third installation created as part of the initiative.

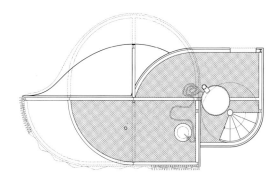

Ground floor

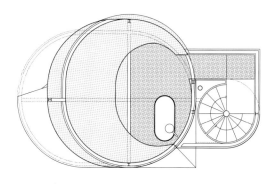

Second floor

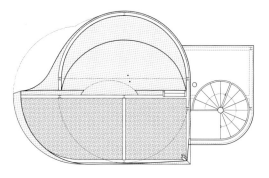

Third floor

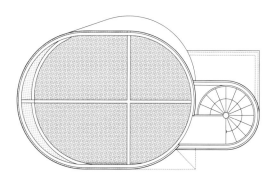

Fourth floor

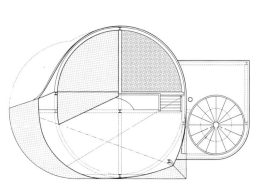

Fifth floor

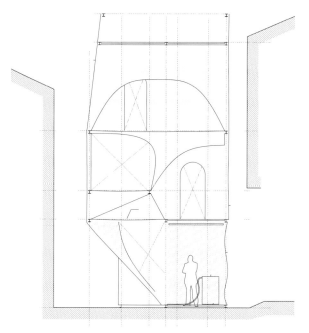

Section

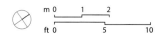

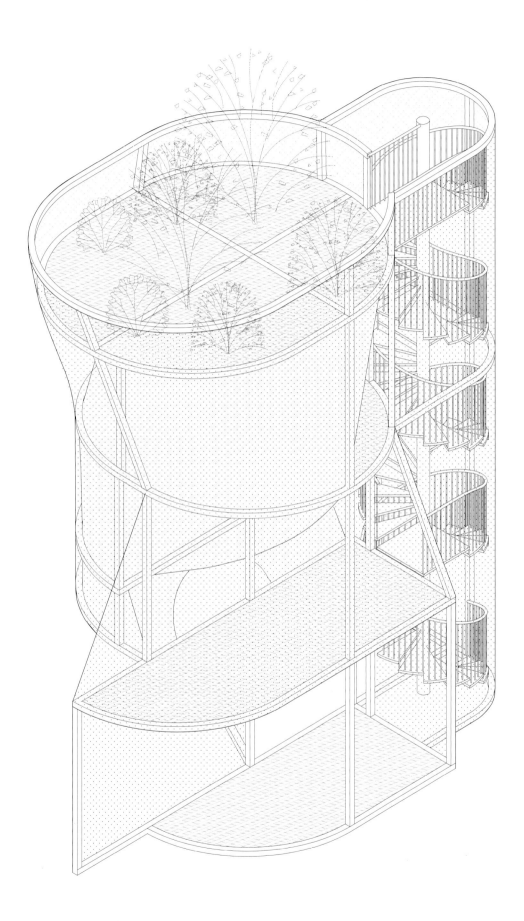

Axonometric

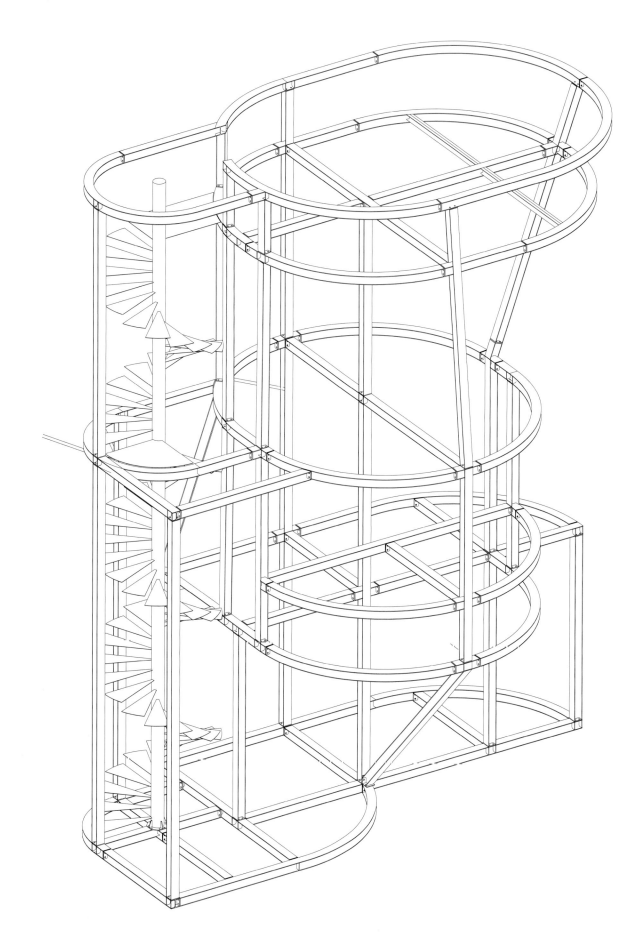

Structural diagram

Florian Idenburg & Ana Prvački.
Courtesy of SO – IL.

About Ana Prvački:
In her videos, services, concoctions, and drawings, Ana
Prvački uses a gently pedagogical and comedic approach
in an attempt to reconcile etiquette and erotics. She aims for
a conceptual practice with a low carbon footprint.

DATE: September 2017 / LOCATION: Chicago Architecture Biennial 2017 / TEAM: Florian idenburg, Jing Liu, Ilias Papageorgiou Seunghyun Kang (Project Lead), Anna Margit, Diandra Rendradjaja, Yan Ma, Qionglu Lei, Sophie Nichols, Iason Houssein / COLLABORATOR: Ana Prvački / PHOTOS: Iwan Baan

L'air pour l'air

Chicago Architecture Biennial 2017

In conjunction with "Making New History," the second edition of the Chicago Architecture Biennial, SO – IL and artist Ana Prvački presented for the first time a special project during the Biennial's opening week last September. Titled "L'air pour l'air," the project aimed to ensure the continued legacy of musicians as our cities' atmospheres grow more polluted.

Inspired by the abundant plant life in the Garfield Park Conservatory, SO – IL and Prvački have created an ensemble of air-filtering mesh enclosures, designed to clean the air through breathing. Part mask, part shelter, the enclosures were worn by an ensemble of saxophone, flute, trombone, and vocals from the Chicago Sinfonietta. Through performing an original composition, *De Aere* (concerning the air), by composer Veronika Krausas, the musicians 'cleaned the air that produces the music.' The installation and performance encouraged its viewers to meditate upon the complex notions such as the relationship between purity and pollution, and the distinctions between self, body, objects, and nature.

Enlightening visitors' senses has been a consistent endeavor of SO – IL. Prior to "L'air pour l'air," they created "Passage," a reflection on the spatial qualities of the ramp, for the Chicago Architecture Biennial in 2015. In response to a perceived incline and distance, one's navigational sense corrects one's movement by adjusting pace and posture. This installation endeavors to interrupt this automatic response by heightening an awareness of one's body in space. The Biennial selected "Passage" to remain on site, which is now on view at the Chicago Cultural Center.

L'air pour l'air | A walking meditation for quartet

veronika krausas

text by **Hildegard von Bingen**
English translation by **Tom Sapsford**

Commissioned by **Ana Prvački** & **Florian Idenburg**
L'air pour l'air for 2017 Chicago Architecture Biennial

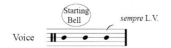

Performance Note: The bell and each intial incipit signal the move to a new section.
Sections may be performed in any order and portions of each repeated ad lib performers.